THE FABER BOOK
OF
LOVE POEMS

The Faber Book of
LOVE POEMS

Love Expected ❧ Love Begun ❧
The Plagues of Loving ❧
Love Continued ❧ Absences,
Doubts, Division ❧
Love Renounced & Love in Death

EDITED WITH AN INTRODUCTION BY

Geoffrey Grigson

faber and faber
LONDON · BOSTON

First published in 1973
by Faber and Faber Limited
3 Queen Square London WC1N 3AU
This paperback edition first published in 1983

Printed and bound in Great Britain by
Mackays of Chatham PLC, Chatham, Kent
All rights reserved

Introduction and this selection
© Geoffrey Grigson, 1973

A CIP record for this book
is available from the British Library

ISBN 0 571 13118 2

13 15 17 19 18 16 14

TO JANE

CONTENTS

INTRODUCTION

There are love poems, in-love poems, that is to say, and poems about love. Both have been included in this collection, but not one for one. The in-love poems are more numerous, as they should be. They are the poems of situation, drama, instantaneity. I love you, or I long for you and you don't love me, or we love each other, isn't it wonderful, or we have to separate, what misery for us, or I love you for ever, or I write this poem about you in which our loving each other and your exquisiteness will be embalmed in spices of image and sound. Or you reject me, and I return, with whatever reluctance and relief, to my senses, and reject love. For the time being.

Always an I and You. And of course one's thought about such poems scurries straightaway to 'It was the lark, the herald of the morn' or across another four centuries to Provene, to the alba, the poem of the night of love and then the white dawn (which is what *alba* first means) and the watchman who calls out that the day is showing—in fact to the one particular, famous alba (so well translated by Ezra Pound, No. 194):

> Oy Dieus, oy Dieus, de l'alba! tan tast ve.
> Ah God! How swift the night,?
> And day comes on!

It was a cosy idea, it was a special pink feather in the modern European cap, that Provençal song-makers had invented the love lyric, which corresponded to the new *amour courtois*, the new mutuality of tenderness, which had been invented in the South all of a sudden at the beginning of the twelfth century. Historians of literature and love, or literature and culture, have altered that. As they say, there are Chinese albas—at any rate two of them, surviving—written about twenty-five centuries ago, in which lovers are warned by a damnable rooster that the affairs of day have arrived, or are about to arrive, with dawn (Arthur Waley translated them, but I suppose necessarily into that thin line by line prose which now passes too easily for poems: they are Numbers 25 and 26 in his version of *The Book of Songs*); and there is an Egyptian lyric, too, thirty-three centuries old, in which a swallow warns the girl in bed with her lover that it is almost day. Of course specialists now rightly say that the situations which instigate an alba, or any other kind of in-love poem, or You and I poem, are elemental.

'The feelings and conceptions of *amour courtois*', Peter Dronke writes, 'are universally possible', anywhere, at any time, at any social level.

'They occur in popular as well as in learned or aristocratic love poetry. Like Dante in the fourth book of the *Convivio*, I hold that here is a *gentilezza* which is not confined to any court or privileged class, but springs from an inherent virtù; that the feelings of *courtoisie* are elemental. In the poet's terms, they allow even the most *vilain* to be *gentil*.' (*Medieval Latin and the Rise of European Love-Lyric*, 1968.)

Good. I happened to read in the same few days Peter Dronke's book and that letter William de Morgan picked up on the beach at Sidmouth in 1887, written by a nearly illiterate worker on a farm to his 'Dearest Mary pure and holey meek and loly lovely Rose of Sharon', an exclamation he repeated three times like a refrain (for *that* writer no illusion that the 'Song of Solomon' was allegorical, and not a straight love poem).[1]

But there it is. The silliest things are often said about or against the conventional circumstances which so very widely shape the poems of being in love. But the conventions—think of your own life—derive from the happenings. And there is no such situation in love poems which is not grounded—like the myths of Aphrodite and her blind arrow-shooting child, so conveniently popularized and employed again since the Renaissance—in the psychology and etiology of love. Love is less hedged than it was. But hedges can still be thorny and difficult. Drain-pipes are—still—climbed to windows. One may act—still—as though one had been hit by a sudden arrow of humiliating insanity. Cocks continue to crow in the morning, swallows to chatter; it continues to be possible to hear nightingales, and then larks with the whitening of the sky and the separation which has to follow. Or if things never get so far, or have been reversed, doors may not be opened.

> Let me not, for pity, more,
> Tell the long hours at your door.

Imagine this, experience it, if you have to, high up in a tower of flats—

> Do not mock me in thy bed
> While these cold nights freeze me dead.

Or experience this—you might have to, after all—by a gangway to a cold houseboat or outside a closed caravan.

---

[1] 'In Hebrew it remains to our day the supreme model for all poetry of this genre, and any study of erotic poetry in that language must take it as a starting-point.' Professor J. B. Segal in A. T. Hatto's *Eos: An Enquiry into the Theme of Lovers' Meetings and Partings at Dawn in Poetry*, The Hague, 1965.

What never impresses me is some chilly statement that a poem having great powers to move and to possess—say a particular sonnet by Ronsard or Drayton—was, or was likely to have been, an exercise simply, by a great artist. Poems which have such power cannot be compelled into existence by anything except situations—states of ecstasy, states of anguish, states of happiness, confusion, chaos of feelings, et cetera—which have been lived through, however customary are the incidents and externals of the poem.

An example. Sir Philip Sidney's latest editor, William A. Ringler, Jr.,[1] feels—no, thinks—that 'Leave me, O Love, which reachest but to dust' (No. 356) wasn't the outcome of having been in love, so irrationally in the nature of the business, and hopelessly, with Lady Rich, the Stella of his grand *Astrophel and Stella*. He goes on from his argument that this renouncing of love was written earlier than *Astrophel and Stella* (for this the evidence is circumstantial, not watertight) to remark that 'Sidney was just as capable as any other poet of writing about a number of mistresses real *or imaginary*'. (The italics of decided disagreement are mine.)

If one knows about the writing of poems, such a poem as Sidney's, of such quality, cannot be conceived as an exercise to do with fancied circumstances.

The wonderful graveness of Sidney's poem (so important to him, one may think, that he gave it a postscript in very resonant Latin) was the consequence, within its convention, surely of a storm of love, for someone, whether Penelope Rich or a girl we know nothing about (myself, I think it unlikely—setting one thing against another—that Sidney ever loved two girls, within a short time, one of them to the pitch of the whole of *Astrophel and Stella*, one to the ultimate pitch of 'Leave me, O love').

Roundabout, then, I reach this point: that poets *mean* good poems of the kind we are discussing. They write these poems for themselves, in the first place; and only in-loveness, or its recollection, begets in such poems Valéry's 'state of song', which we must continue to understand is the proper state of poetry. It is only that condition of pain, pleasure and derangement which can produce, but in the right poet, the lyric at once dramatic and instantaneous and so enchainingly melodic.

Love isn't everything, but it has had a long history, in Peter Dronke's sense of it, and being immersed in love does rev up and release an energy, does cause the poet to invent, to discover, to relate, in words, in particulars, in movement; his cognizance is suddenly brightened,

[1] *The Poems of Sir Philip Sidney*, 1962.

his share of the world is suddenly enlarged. So his love poems are likely to be equal with a poet's best. Being in love, lasting only a short time, can raise a not so good poet to his one or two good lyrics, even to his one or two good lines. Several poems in this collection reduce themselves to an exceptional line or two, such as 'I saw my love younger than primroses' (No. 132), 'Love still has something of the sea' (No. 31), 'Cupid and my Campaspe played' (No. 110), or (No. 143)

> King Pandion, he is dead,
> All thy friends are lapp'd in lead.

It can be deceptive, encountering such lines. For instance, when I first discovered 'The Outlaw of Loch Lene' (No. 123), by J. J. Callanan, I dug out his two uncommon books, naïvely sure that there must be other such lines by him as 'The birds go to sleep by the sweet wild twist of her song'.

There weren't; and one comes to realize that there is not a prodigality of good verse, that there are minor poets who live in a stanza, and much publicized poets who remain dead in five thick collected volumes (with scholar's apparatus). Certainly poetry devoid of love poems is inconceivable; and to think only of single lines again, how many in our own poetry that we could least do without have been due to the interaction of love and the right poet. It would be easy to anthologize this anthology (which readers will no doubt do, in any case), to pick out the lines—

> 'O, my love, my love is young!'
> 'O grey-leafy pinks o' the geärden'
> 'In his green den the murmuring seal'
> 'When our furrows snow shall cover'
> 'Is love's bed always snow?'
> 'Upon this Primrose Hill'
> 'What fair pomp have I spied of glittering ladies?'
> 'Quondam was I. She said for ever'
> 'I hear a cry of spirits faint and blind'

But where should one stop?

I reflect it is thirty-three centuries since the making of that Egyptian alba[1] in which the girl exclaims that she has found her darling on his bed, and that if our own time, for various reasons, is stingy with love poems or poems about love, stingy in fact with the cadences of poetry, the taste cannot have vanished, the situations persist, and are likely to persist, if we don't ruin and burn ourselves, for another thirty-three centuries. And since poets are celebrated for their failure to escape—

[1] Text and translation are given in *Eos*.

'I must love her, that loves not me'—we haven't finished yet with the poet's attempt to solace himself, in the chaos of being in love, by firmly enclosing as much of it as he can in measure:

> Then as th'earth's inward narrow crooked lanes
> Do purge sea water's fretful salt away,
>   I thought, if I could draw my pains
> Through rhyme's vexations, I should them allay,
> Grief brought to numbers cannot be so fierce,
> For, he tames it, that fetters it in verse.
>
> (No. 148)

There will be more love poets to add—many more—to Donne, Clare, Drayton, Wyatt, Sidney, Barnes, Christina Rossetti, Robert Graves.

Two other things. In spite of my quotation above from Peter Dronke I have included next to no popular love poetry, in the shape of ballads, songs, etc. The assembled pick of them is easy to come by in several collections, and a book cannot go on and on. But I shall not apologize for having included a handful at any rate of French poems. French poets have been our historical neighbours in the art, and not infrequently our instructors. Some readers who may not have met them, are going to be grateful, let us say, for reading 'Qu'en avez-vous fait' (No. 339) or that wonder work of popular song 'Sur les Marches du palais' (No. 122). What I have not included—we have too much of it now for the health of our taste in poetry—is the un-measured, thin-rolled short crust of translation (Chinese, Japanese, Polish, Russian, and so on), useful, but now so easily accepted in itself as verse.

GEOFFREY GRIGSON

I

LOVE EXPECTED

1 THE REVELATION

An idle poet, here and there,
    Looks round him; but, for all the rest,
The world, unfathomably fair,
    Is duller than a witling's jest.
Love wakes men, once a lifetime each;
    They lift their heavy lids, and look;
And, lo, what one sweet page can teach,
    They read with joy, then shut the book.
And some give thanks, and some blaspheme
    And most forget; but, either way,
That and the Child's unheeded dream
Is all the light of all their day.

COVENTRY PATMORE

2 BEAUTY AND LOVE

Beauty and love are all my dream;
    They change not with the changing day;
Love stays forever like a stream
    That flows but never flows away;

And beauty is the bright sun-bow
    That blossoms on the spray that showers
Where the loud water falls below,
    Making a wind among the flowers.

ANDREW YOUNG

And therefore take the present time.
With a hey, and a ho, and a hey nonino,
For love is crowned with the prime.
    In spring time, the only pretty ring time,
    When birds do sing, hey ding a ding, ding.
    Sweet lovers love the spring.

WILLIAM SHAKESPEARE

6 A SPRING MORNING

The Spring comes in with all her hues and smells,
In freshness breathing over hills and dells;
O'er woods where May her gorgeous drapery flings,
And meads washed fragrant by their laughing springs.
Fresh are new opened flowers, untouched and free
From the bold rifling of the amorous bee.
The happy time of singing birds is come,
And Love's lone pilgrimage now finds a home;
Among the mossy oaks now coos the dove,
And the hoarse crow finds softer notes for love.
The foxes play around their dens, and bark
In joy's excess, 'mid woodland shadows dark.
The flowers join lips below; the leaves above;
And every sound that meets the ear is Love.

JOHN CLARE

7 IN THE SPRING

My love is the maïd ov all maïdens,
    Though all mid be comely,
Her skin's lik' the jessamy blossom
    A-spread in the Spring.

— O fils du Roi tu es méchant
D'avoir tué mon canard blanc!

Tu me le paieras cinq cents francs
Que ferons-nous de cet argent?
Nous ferons bâtir un couvent
Pour mettr' les fill' de dix-huit ans

Et les garçons de vingt-cinq ans.

5

It was a lover, and his lass,
With a hey, and a ho, and a hey nonino,
That o'er the green corn field did pass,
  In the spring time, the only pretty ring time,
  When birds do sing, hey ding a ding, ding.
  Sweet lovers love the spring.

Between the acres of the rye,
With a hey, and a ho, and a hey nonino,
Those pretty country folks would lie,
  In spring time, the only pretty ring time,
  When birds do sing, hey ding a ding, ding.
  Sweet lovers love the spring.

This carol they began that hour,
With a hey, and a ho, and a hey nonino:
How that a life was but a flower,
  In spring time, the only pretty ring time,
  When birds do sing, hey ding a ding, ding.
  Sweet lovers love the spring.

And therefore take the present time.
With a hey, and a ho, and a hey nonino,
For love is crowned with the prime.
   In spring time, the only pretty ring time,
   When birds do sing, hey ding a ding, ding.
   Sweet lovers love the spring.

WILLIAM SHAKESPEARE

6 A SPRING MORNING

The Spring comes in with all her hues and smells,
In freshness breathing over hills and dells;
O'er woods where May her gorgeous drapery flings,
And meads washed fragrant by their laughing springs.
Fresh are new opened flowers, untouched and free
From the bold rifling of the amorous bee.
The happy time of singing birds is come,
And Love's lone pilgrimage now finds a home;
Among the mossy oaks now coos the dove,
And the hoarse crow finds softer notes for love.
The foxes play around their dens, and bark
In joy's excess, 'mid woodland shadows dark.
The flowers join lips below; the leaves above;
And every sound that meets the ear is Love.

JOHN CLARE

7 IN THE SPRING

My love is the maïd ov all maïdens,
   Though all mid be comely,
Her skin's lik' the jessamy blossom
   A-spread in the Spring.

I THE REVELATION

An idle poet, here and there,
  Looks round him; but, for all the rest,
The world, unfathomably fair,
  Is duller than a witling's jest.
Love wakes men, once a lifetime each;
  They lift their heavy lids, and look;
And, lo, what one sweet page can teach,
  They read with joy, then shut the book.
And some give thanks, and some blaspheme
  And most forget; but, either way,
That and the Child's unheeded dream
Is all the light of all their day.

COVENTRY PATMORE

2 BEAUTY AND LOVE

Beauty and love are all my dream;
  They change not with the changing day;
Love stays forever like a stream
  That flows but never flows away;

And beauty is the bright sun-bow
  That blossoms on the spray that showers
Where the loud water falls below,
  Making a wind among the flowers.

ANDREW YOUNG

3

In a herber green, asleep whereas I lay,
The birds sang sweet in the middes of the day,
I dreamed fast of mirth and play,
In youth is pleasure, in youth is pleasure.

Methought as I walked still to and fro,
And from her company I could not go,
But when I waked it was not so,
In youth is pleasure, in youth is pleasure.

Therefore my heart is surely pight,
Of her alone to have a sight,
Which is my joy and heart's delight,
In youth is pleasure, in youth is pleasure.

ROBERT WEVER

4 LE CANARD BLANC

(FOLKSONG)

Derrière nous, y a un étang
N'est pas si creux comme il est grand
Trois beaux canards y vont nageant
Y en a deux noirs, y en a un blanc

Le fils du Roi s'en va chassant
Avec son beau fusil d'argent
Mire le noir et tue le blanc
Toute la plum' s'envole au vent

Trois dam' vont la ramassant
C'est pour en faire un beau lit blanc

Her smile is so sweet as a beäby's
  Young smile on his mother,
Her eyes be as bright as the dew drop
  A-shed in the Spring.

O grey-leafy pinks o' the geärden,
  Now bear her sweet blossoms;
Now deck wi' a rwose-bud, O briar,
  Her head in the Spring.

O light-rollen wind, blow me hither
  The vaïce ov her talken,
Or bring vrom her veet the light doust
  She do tread in the Spring.

O zun, meäke the gil'cups all glitter,
  In goold all around her;
An' meäke o' the deäisies' white flowers
  A bed in the Spring.

O whissle, gaÿ birds, up bezide her,
  In drong-way an' woodlands,
O zing, swingen lark, now the clouds
  Be a-vled in the Spring.

An' who, you mid ax, be my praïses
  A-meäken so much o'?
An' oh! 'tis the maïd I'm a-hopen
  To wed in the Spring.

WILLIAM BARNES

8 LOVE WILL FIND OUT THE WAY

Over the mountains
  And under the waves,
Over the fountains
  And under the graves,
Over floods which are the deepest
  Which do Neptune obey,
Over rocks which are steepest,
  Love will find out the way.

Where there is no place
  For the glow-worm to lie;
Where there is no space
  For receipt of a fly;
Where the gnat she dares not venter,
  Lest herself fast she lay;
But if Love come, he will enter,
  And will find out the way.

You may esteem him
  A child by his force,
Or you may deem him
  A coward, which is worse;
But if he whom Love doth honour
  Be concealed from the day,
Set a thousand guards upon him,
  Love will find out the way.

Some think to lose him,
  Which is too unkind;
And some do suppose him,
  Poor heart, to be blind;
If that he were hidden,
  Do the best that you may,
Blind Love, if so you call him,
  Will find out the way.

Well may the eagle
  Stoop down to the fist;
Or you may inveigle
  The phœnix of the east;
With fear the tiger's moved
  To give over his prey,
But never stop a lover,
  He will post on his way.

From Dover to Berwick,
  And nations throughout,
Brave Guy of Warwick,
  That champion so stout,
With his warlike behaviour,
  Through the world he did stray
To win his Phyllis' favour—
  Love will find out the way.

In order next enters
  Bevis so brave;
After adventures,
  And policy grave,
To see whom he desired,
  His Josian so gay,
For whom his heart was fired,
  Love found out the way.

The Gordian knot
  Which true lovers knit,
Undo you cannot,
  Nor yet break it;
Make use of your inventions
  Their fancies to betray,
To frustrate your intentions
  Love will find out the way.

From court to the cottage,
　　In bower and in hall,
From the king unto the beggar,
　　Love conquers all;
Though ne'er so stout and lordly,
　　Strive, do what you may,
Yet, be you ne'er so hardy,
　　Love will find out the way.

Love hath power over princes
　　And greatest emperor;
In any provinces,
　　Such is Love's power,
There is no resisting,
　　But him to obey;
In spite of all contesting,
　　Love will find out the way.

If that he were hidden,
　　And all men that are,
Were strictly forbidden
　　That place to declare,
Winds that have no abidings,
　　Pitying their delay,
Will come and bring him tidings,
　　And direct him the way.

If the earth should part him
　　He would gallop it o'er;
If the seas should o'erthwart him,
　　He would swim to the shore;
Should his love become a swallow,
　　Through the air to stray,
Love would lend wings to follow,
　　And will find out the way.

There is no striving
  To cross his intent,
There is no contriving
  His plots to prevent;
But if once the message greet him
  That his true love doth stay,
If death should come and meet him,
  Love will find out the way.

ANON.

9 A REPORT SONG IN A DREAM, BETWEEN A SHEPHERD AND HIS NYMPH

Shall we go dance the hay? The hay?
Never pipe could ever play
  Better shepherd's roundelay.

Shall we go sing the song? The song?
Never love did ever wrong:
  Fair maids hold hands all along.

Shall we go learn to woo? To woo?
Never thought came ever to
  Better deed, could better do.

Shall we go learn to kiss? To kiss?
Never heart could ever miss
  Comfort, where true meaning is.

Thus at base they run, They run,
When the sport was scarce begun:
  But I waked, and all was done.

NICHOLAS BRETON

10 [THE SYRENS' SONG]

Steer hither, steer, your winged pines,
    All beaten mariners,
Here lie Love's undiscover'd mines,
    A prey to passengers;
Perfumes far sweeter than the best
Which make the Phoenix' urn and nest.
    Fear not your ships,
Nor any to oppose you save our lips,
    But come on shore
Where no joy dies till love hath gotten more.

    But come on shore
Where no joy dies till love hath gotten more.

For swelling waves, our panting breasts
    Where never storms arise,
Exchange; and be awhile our guests:
    For stars gaze on our eyes.
The compass love shall hourly sing,
And as he goes about the ring,
    We will not miss
To tell each point he nameth with a kiss.

    Then come on shore,
Where no joy dies till love hath gotten more.

WILLIAM BROWNE OF TAVISTOCK

11 SONG

Choose now among this fairest number,
Upon whose breasts love would for ever slumber:
Choose not amiss since you may where you will,
    Or blame yourself for choosing ill.

Then do not leave, though oft the music closes,
Till lilies in their cheeks be turn'd to roses.

WILLIAM BROWNE OF TAVISTOCK

12 THE UNKNOWN

She is most fair,
And when they see her pass
The poets' ladies
Look no more in the glass
But after her.

On a bleak moor
Running under the moon
She lures a poet,
Once proud or happy, soon
Far from his door.

Beside a train,
Because they saw her go,
Or failed to see her,
Travellers and watchers know
Another pain.

The simple lack
Of her is more to me
Than others' presence,
Whether life splendid be
Or utter black.

I have not seen,
I have no news of her;
I can tell only
She is not here, but there
She might have been.

She is to be kissed
Only perhaps by me;
She may be seeking
Me and no other; she
May not exist.

EDWARD THOMAS

13 LE MANCHY

Sous un nuage frais de claire mousseline,
    Tous les dimanches au matin,
Tu venais à la ville en manchy de rotin,
    Par les rampes de la colline.

La cloche de l'église alertement tintait;
    Le vent de mer berçait les cannes;
Comme une grêle d'or, aux pointes des savanes,
    Le feu du soleil crépitait.

Le bracelet aux poings, l'anneau sur la cheville,
    Et le mouchoir jaune aux chignons,
Deux Telingas portaient, assidus compagnons,
    Ton lit aux nattes de Manille.

Ployant leur jarret maigre et nerveux, et chantant,
    Souples dans leurs tuniques blanches,
Le bambou sur l'épaule et les mains sur les hanches,
    Ils allaient le long de l'Étang.

Le long de la chaussée et des varangues basses
    Où les vieux créoles fumaient,
Par les groupes joyeux des Noirs, ils s'animaient
    Au bruit des bobres Madécasses.

Dans l'air léger flottait l'odeur des tamarins;
  Sur les houles illuminées,
Au large, les oiseaux, en d'immenses traînées,
  Plongeaient dans les brouillards marins.

Et tandis que ton pied, sorti de la babouche,
  Pendait, rose, au bord du manchy,
A l'ombre des Bois-noirs touffus, et du Letchi
  Aux fruits moins pourprés que ta bouche;

Tandis qu'un papillon, les deux ailes en fleur,
  Teinté d'azur et d'écarlate,
Se posait par instants sur ta peau délicate
  En y laissant de sa couleur;

On voyait, au travers du rideau de batiste,
  Tes boucles dorer l'oreiller,
Et, sous leurs cils mi-clos, feignant de sommeiller,
  Tes beaux yeux de sombre améthyste.

Tu t'en venais ainsi, par ces matins si doux,
  De la montagne à la grand'messe,
Dans ta grace naïve et ta rose jeunesse,
  Au pas rythmé de tes Hindous.

Maintenant, dans le sable aride de nos grêves,
  Sous le chiendents, au bruit des mers,
Tu reposes parmi les morts qui me sont chers,
  O charme de mes premiers rêves!

CHARLES-MARIE LECONTE DE LISLE

14

There is a lady sweet and kind,
Was never face so pleas'd my mind,
I did but see her passing by,
And yet I love her till I die.

Her gesture, motion and her smiles,
Her wit, her voice my heart beguiles,
Beguiles my heart, I know not why,
And yet I love her till I die.

Her free behaviour, winning looks,
Will make a lawyer burn his books.
I touch'd her not, alas not I,
And yet I love her till I die.

Had I her fast betwixt mine arms,
Judge you that think such sports were harms,
Wert any harm? no, no, fie, fie,
For I will love her till I die.

Should I remain confined there,
So long as Phoebus in his sphere,
I to request, she to deny,
Yet would I love her till I die.

Cupid is winged and doth range,
Her country so my love doth change,
But change she earth, or change she sky,
Yet will I love her till I die.

ANON.

15 FANTAISIE

Il est un air pour qui je donnerais
Tout Rossini, tout Mozart et tout Weber
Un air très vieux, languissant et funèbre,
Qui pour moi seul a des charmes secrets.

Or, chaque fois que je viens à l'entendre,
De deux cents ans mon âme rajeunit:—
C'est sous Louis treize; et je crois voir s'étendre
Un coteau vert, que le couchant jaunit.

Puis un château de brique à coins de pierre,
Aux vitraux teints de rougeâtres couleurs,
Ceint de grands parcs, avec une rivière
Baignant ses pieds, qui coule entre des fleurs;

Puis une dame, à sa haute fenêtre,
Blonde aux yeux noirs, en ses habits anciens,
Que, dans une autre existence peut-être,
J'ai déjà vue… — et dont je me souviens!

GÉRARD DE NERVAL

16 THE MERMAIDENS' VESPER-HYMN

Troop home to silent grots and caves!
    Troop home! and mimic as you go
The mournful winding of the waves
    Which to their dark abysses flow.

At this sweet hour, all things beside
    In amorous pairs to covert creep;
The swans that brush the evening tide
    Homeward in snowy couples keep.

In his green den the murmuring seal
  Close by his sleek companion lies;
While singly we to bedward steal,
  And close in fruitless sleep our eyes.

In bowers of love men take their rest,
  In loveless bowers we sigh alone,
With bosom friends are others blest, —
  But we have none! but we have none!

GEORGE DARLEY

17 I HID MY LOVE

I hid my love when young till I
Couldn't bear the buzzing of a fly;
I hid my love to my despite
Till I could not bear to look at light:
I dare not gaze upon her face
But left her memory in each place;
Where'er I saw a wild flower lie
I kissed and bade my love good-bye.

I met her in the greenest dells,
Where dewdrops pearl the wood bluebells;
The lost breeze kissed her bright blue eye,
The bee kissed and went singing by,
A sunbeam found a passage there,
A gold chain round her neck so fair;
As secret as the wild bee's song
She lay there all the summer long.

I hid my love in field and town
Till e'en the breeze would knock me down;
The bees seemed singing ballads o'er,
The fly's bass turned a lion's roar;

And even silence found a tongue,
To haunt me all the summer long;
The riddle nature could not prove
Was nothing else but secret love.

JOHN CLARE

18 ADOLESCENCE

J'allais au Luxembourg rêver, ô temps lointain,
Dès l'aurore, et j'étais moi-même le matin.
Les nids dialoguaient tout bas, et les allées
Désertes étaient d'ombre et de soleil mêlées;
J'étais pensif, j'étais profond, j'étais niais.
Comme je regardais et comme j'épiais!
Qui? La Vénus, l'Hébé, la nymphe chasseresse.
Je sentais du printemps l'invisible caresse.
Je guettais l'inconnu. J'errais. Quel curieux
Que Chérubin en qui s'éveille Des Grieux!
O femme! mystère! être ignoré qu'on encense!
Parfois j'étais obscène à force d'innocence.
Mon regard violait la vague nudité
Des déesses, debout sous les feuilles l'été;
Je contemplais de loin ces rondeurs peu vêtues,
Et j'étais amoureux de toutes les statues;
Et j'en ai mis plus d'une en colère, je crois.
Les audaces dans l'ombre égalent les effrois,
Et, hardi comme un page et tremblant comme un lièvre,
Oubliant latin, grec, algèbre, ayant la fièvre
Qui résiste aux Bezouts et brave les Restauds,
Je restais la stupide au bas des piédestaux,
Comme si j'attendais que le vent sous quelque arbre
Soulevât les jupons d'une Diane en marbre.

VICTOR HUGO

Silly boy, 'tis full moon yet, thy night as day shines clearly;
Had thy youth but wit to fear, thou couldst not love so dearly.
Shortly wilt thou mourn when all thy pleasures are bereaved;
Little knows he how to love that never was deceived.

This is thy first maiden flame, that triumphs yet unstained;
All is artless now you speak, not one word yet is fained;
All is heav'n that you behold, and all your thoughts are blessed:
But no Spring can want his Fall, each Troilus hath his Cressid.

Thy well-order'd locks ere long shall rudely hang neglected;
And thy lively pleasant cheer read grief on earth dejected.
Much then wilt thou blame thy Saint, that made thy heart so holy,
And with sighs confess, in love, that too much faith is folly.

Yet, be just and constant still; Love may beget a wonder,
Not unlike a Summer's frost, or Winter's fatal thunder:
He that holds his sweetheart true unto his day of dying
Lives, of all that ever breath'd, most worthy the envying.

THOMAS CAMPION

20 [HERO FEELS THE SHAFT OF LOVE, *from*
'HERO AND LEANDER']

'Gentle youth, forbear
To touch the sacred garments which I wear.
Upon a rock, and underneath a hill,
Far from the town (where all is whist and still,
Save that the sea playing on yellow sand,
Sends forth a rattling murmur to the land,
Whose sound allures the golden Morpheus
In silence of the night to visit us)

My turret stands, and there God knows I play
With Venus' swans and sparrows all the day.
A dwarfish beldame bears me company,
That hops about the chamber where I lie,
And spends the night (that might be better spent)
In vain discourse, and apish merriment.
Come thither.' As she spake this, her tongue tripped,
For unawares 'Come thither' from her slipped,
And suddenly her former colour changed,
And here and there her eyes through anger ranged.
And like a planet, moving several ways,
At one self instant, she poor soul assays,
Loving, not to love at all, and every part
Strove to resist the motions of her heart.
And hands so pure, so innocent, nay such,
As might have made heaven stoop to have a touch,
Did she uphold to Venus, and again
Vowed spotless chastity, but all in vain.
Cupid beats down her prayers with his wings,
Her vows above the empty air he flings:
All deep enraged, his sinewy bow he bent,
And shot a shaft that burning from him went,
Wherewith she strooken looked so dolefully,
As made Love sigh, to see his tyranny.
And as she wept, her tears to pearl he turned,
And wound them on his arm, and for her mourned.

CHRISTOPHER MARLOWE

21

Would I were chang'd into that golden shower
   That so divinely streamed from the skies,
To fall in drops upon my dainty flower
   When in her bed she solitary lies.

Then would I hope such showers as richly shine
Should pierce more deep than these waste tears of mine.

Else would I were that plumed swan snow-white
   Under whose form was hidden heavenly power.
Then in that river would I most delight
   Whose waves do beat against her stately bower
And on those banks so tune my dying song
That her deaf ears should think my plaints too long.

Or would I were Narcissus, that sweet boy,
   And she her self the fountain crystal clear,
Who ravish'd with the pride of his own joy,
   Drenched his limbs with gazing over near.
So should I bring my soul to happy rest
To end my life in that I loved best.

SIR ARTHUR GORGES

22 RÊVÉ POUR L'HIVER

A . . . ELLE

L'hiver, nous irons dans un petit wagon rose
   Avec des coussins bleus.
Nous serons bien. Un nid de baisers fous repose
   Dans chaque coin moelleux.

Tu fermeras l'œil, pour ne point voir, par la glace,
   Grimacer les ombres des soirs,
Ces monstruosités hargneuses, populace
   De démons noirs et de loups noirs.

Puis tu te sentiras la joue égratignée . . .
Un petit baiser, comme une folle araignée,
   Te courra par le cou . . .

Et tu me diras: «Cherche!» en inclinant la tête,
—Et nous prendrons du temps à trouver cette bête
   —Qui voyage beaucoup...

ARTHUR RIMBAUD

23   A DREAM

Was it a dream? We sailed, I thought we sailed,
Martin and I, down a green Alpine stream,
Bordered, each bank, with pines; the morning sun,
On the wet umbrage of their glossy tops,
On the red pinings of their forest-floor,
Drew a warm scent abroad; behind the pines
The mountain-skirts, with all their sylvan change
Of bright-leafed chestnuts and mossed walnut-trees
And the frail scarlet-berried ash, began.
Swiss chalets glittered on the dewy slopes,
And from some swarded shelf, high up, there came,
Notes of wild pastoral music—over all
Ranged, diamond-bright, the eternal wall of snow.
Upon the mossy rocks at the stream's edge,
Backed by the pines, a plank-built cottage stood,
Bright in the sun; the climbing gourd-plant's leaves
Muffled its walls, and on the stone-strewn roof
Lay the warm golden gourds; golden, within,
Under the eaves, peered rows of Indian corn.
We shot beneath the cottage with the stream.
On the brown, rude-carved balcony, two forms
Came forth—Olivia's, Marguerite! and thine.
Clad were they both in white, flowers in their breast;
Straw hats bedecked their heads, with ribbons blue,
Which danced, and on their shoulders, fluttering, played.

They saw us, they conferred; their bosoms heaved,
And more than mortal impulse filled their eyes.
Their lips moved; their white arms, waved eagerly,
Flashed once, like falling streams; we rose, we gazed.
One moment, on the rapid's top, our boat
Hung poised—and then the darting river of Life
(Such now, methought, it was), the river of Life,
Loud thundering, bore us by; swift, swift it foamed,
Black under cliffs it raced, round headlands shone.
Soon the planked cottage by the sun-warmed pines
Faded—the moss—the rocks; us burning plains,
Bristled with cities, us the sea received.

MATTHEW ARNOLD

24

Bright Star! would I were steadfast as thou art—
Not in lone splendour hung aloft the night,
And watching, with eternal lids apart,
Like Nature's patient sleepless Eremite,
The moving waters at their priestlike task
Of pure ablution round earth's human shores,
Or gazing on the new soft-fallen mask
Of snow upon the mountains and the moors—
No—yet still steadfast, still unchangeable,
Pillowed upon my fair love's ripening breast
To feel for ever its soft fall and swell,
Awake for ever in a sweet unrest;
    Still, still to hear her tender-taken breath,
    And so live ever—or else swoon to death.

JOHN KEATS

25 THE VIGIL OF VENUS
(PERVIGILIUM VENERIS)

I

Tomorrow let loveless, let lover tomorrow make love:
O spring, singing spring, spring of the world renew!
In spring lovers consent and the birds marry
When the grove receives in her hair the nuptial dew.

Tomorrow may loveless, may lover tomorrow make love.

II

Tomorrow's the day when the prime Zeus made love:
Out of lightning foam shot deep in the heaving sea
(Witnessed by green crowds of finny horses)
Dione rising and falling, he made to be!

Tomorrow may loveless, may lover tomorrow make love.

III

Tomorrow the Joiner of love in the gracious shade
Twines her green huts with boughs of myrtle claws,
Tomorrow leads her gangs to the singing woods:
Tomorrow Dione, on high, lays down the laws.

Tomorrow may loveless, may lover tomorrow make love.

IV

She shines the tarnished year with glowing buds
That, wakening, head up to the western wind
In eager clusters. Goddess! You deign to scatter
Lucent night-drip of dew; for you are kind.

Tomorrow may loveless, may lover tomorrow make love.

V

The heavy teardrops stretch, ready to fall,
Then falls each glistening bead to the earth beneath:
The moisture that the serene stars sent down
Loosens the virgin bud from the sliding sheath.

   Tomorrow may loveless, may lover tomorrow make love.

VI

Look, the high crimsons have revealed their shame.
The burning rose turns in her secret bed,
The goddess has bidden the girdle to loose its folds
That the rose at dawn may give her maidenhead.

   Tomorrow may loveless, may lover tomorrow make love.

VII

The blood of Venus enters her blood, Love's kiss
Has made the drowsy virgin modestly bold;
Tomorrow the bride is not ashamed to take
The burning taper from its hidden fold.

   Tomorrow may loveless, may lover tomorrow make love.

VIII

The goddess herself has sent nymphs to the woods,
The Boy with girls to the myrtles; perhaps you think
That Love's not truly tame if he shows his arrows?
Go, girls! Unarmed, Love beckons. You must not shrink.

   Tomorrow may loveless, may lover tomorrow make love.

IX

Bidden unarmed to go and to go naked
Lest he destroy with bow, with dart, with brand—
Yet, girls, Cupid is pretty, and you must know
That Love unarmed can pierce with naked hand!

Tomorrow may loveless, may lover tomorrow make love.

X

Here will be girls of the farm and girls of the mountain
And girls who live by forest, or grove, or spring.
The mother of the Flying Boy has smiled
And said: Now, girls, beware his naked sting!

Tomorrow may loveless, may lover tomorrow make love.

XI

Gently she asks may she bend virginity?
Gently that you, a modest girl, may yield.
Now, should you come, for three nights you would see
Delirious bands in every grove and field.

Tomorrow may loveless, may lover tomorrow make love.

XII

Venus herself has maidens as pure as you;
So, Delia, one thing only we ask: Go away!
That the wood shall not be bloody with slaughtered beasts
When Venus flicks the shadows with greening spray.

Tomorrow may loveless, may lover tomorrow make love.

XIII

Among the garlands, among the myrtle bowers
Ceres and Bacchus, and the god of verse, delay.
Nightlong the watch must be kept with votive cry—
Dione's queen of the woods: Diana, make way!

Tomorrow may loveless, may lover tomorrow make love.

XIV

She places her court among the flowers of Hybla;
Presiding, she speaks her laws; the Graces are near.
Hybla, give all your blossoms, and bring, Hybla,
The brightest plain of Enna for the whole year.

Tomorrow may loveless, may lover tomorrow make love.

XV

With spring the father-sky remakes the world:
The male shower has flowed into the bride,
Earth's body; then shifted through sky and sea and land
To touch the quickening child in her deep side.

Tomorrow may loveless, may lover tomorrow make love.

XVI

Over sky and land and down under the sea
On the path of the seed the goddess brought to earth
And dropped into our veins created fire,
That men might know the mysteries of birth.

Tomorrow may loveless, may lover tomorrow make love.

XVII

Body and mind the inventive Creatress fills
With spirit blowing its invariable power:
The Sabine girls she gave to the sons of Rome
And sowed the seed exiled from the Trojan tower.

Tomorrow may loveless, may lover tomorrow make love.

XVIII

Lavinia of Laurentum she chose to bed
Her son Aeneas, and for the black Mars won
The virgin Silvia, to found the Roman line:
Sire Romulus, and Caesar her grandson.

Tomorrow may loveless, may lover tomorrow make love.

XIX

Venus knows country matters: country knows Venus:
For Love, Dione's boy, was born on the farm.
From the rich furrow she snatched him to her breast,
With tender flowers taught him peculiar charm.

Tomorrow may loveless, may lover tomorrow make love.

XX

See how the bullocks rub their flanks with broom!
See the ram pursue through the shade the bleating ewe,
For lovers' union is Venus in kind pursuit;
And she tells the birds to forget their winter woe.

Tomorrow may loveless, may lover tomorrow make love.

XXI

Now the tall swans with hoarse cries thrash the lake:
The girl of Tereus pours from the poplar ring
Musical change—sad sister who bewails
Her act of darkness with the barbarous king!

Tomorrow may loveless, may lover tomorrow make love.

XXII

She sings, we are silent. When will my spring come?
Shall I find my voice when I shall be as the swallow?
Silence destroyed the Amyclae: they were dumb.
Silent, I lost the muse. Return, Apollo!

Tomorrow let loveless, let lover tomorrow make love.

ANON. (translated from the Latin by ALLEN TATE)

26

'Twas when the spousal time of May
    Hangs all the hedge with bridal wreaths,
And air's so sweet the bosom gay
    Gives thanks for every breath it breathes;
When like to like is gladly moved,
    And each thing joins in Spring's refrain,
'Let those love now who never loved;
    'Let those who have loved love again;'
That I, in whom the sweet time wrought,
    Lay stretch'd within a lonely glade,
Abandon'd to delicious thought,

Beneath the softly twinkling shade.
The leaves, all stirring, mimick'd well
  A neighbouring rush of rivers cold,
And, as the sun or shadow fell,
  So these were green and those were gold;
In dim recesses hyacinths droop'd,
  And breadths of primrose lit the air,
Which, wandering through the woodland, stoop'd
  And gather'd perfumes here and there;
Upon the spray the squirrel swung,
  And careless songsters, six or seven,
Sang lofty songs the leaves among,
  Fit for their only listener, Heaven.

COVENTRY PATMORE

27

Open the door, who's there within?
The fairest of thy mother's kin.
  O come, come, come abroad,
  And hear the shrill birds sing,
  The air with tunes that load.
It is too soon to go to rest,
The sun not midway yet to west.
  The day doth miss thee,
    And will not part
  Until it kiss thee.

Were I as fair as you pretend,
Yet to an unknown seld-seen friend
  I dare not ope the door.
  To hear the sweet birds sing
  Oft proves a dangerous thing.

The sun may run his wonted race,
And yet not gaze on my poor face.
 The day may miss me;
  Therefore depart,
 You shall not kiss me.

ANON.

28

Sweet, Sweet, Sweet, let me go,
What do you mean, to vex me so,
Cease, cease, cease your pleading force,
Do you think thus, to extort remorse,
Now, now, now no more. Alas you overbear me,
And I would cry, but some would hear, I fear me.

ANON.

29

Hot sun, cool fire, temper'd with sweet air,
Black shade, fair nurse, shadow my white hair,
Shine, sun, burn, fire, breathe air and ease me,
Black shade, fair nurse, shroud me and please me;
Shadow (my sweet nurse) keep me from burning,
Make not my glad cause, cause of mourning.
 Let not my beauty's fire
 Enflame unstaid desire,
 Nor pierce any bright eye
 That wand'reth lightly.

GEORGE PEELE

As in the cool-aïr'd road I come by,
                    —in the night,
Under the moon-clim'd height o' the sky,
                    —in the night,
There by the lime's broad lim's as I did staÿ,
While in the aïr dark sheädes wer' at plaÿ
Up on the windor-glass that did keep
Lew vrom the wind, my true love asleep,
                    —in the night.

While in the grey-wall'd height o' the tow'r,
                    —in the night,
Sounded the midnight bell wi' the hour,
                    —in the night,
There come a bright-heäir'd angel that shed
Light vrom her white robe's zilvery thread,
Wi' her vore-vinger held up to meäke
Silence around lest sleepers mid weäke,
                    —in the night.
'Oh! then,' I whisper'd, 'do I behold
                    —in the night.
Linda, my true-love, here in the cwold,
                    —in the night?'
'No,' she meäde answer, 'you do misteäke:
She is asleep, 'tis I be aweäke;
I be her angel brightly a-drest,
Watchèn her slumber while she do rest,
                    —in the night.'

'Zee how the clear win's, brisk in the bough,
                    —in the night,
While they do pass, don't smite on her brow,
                    —in the night;

Zee how the cloud-sheädes naïseless do zweep
Over the house-top where she's asleep.
You, too, goo on, though times mid be near,
When you, wi' me, mid speäk to her ear
                                        —in the night.'

WILLIAM BARNES

31 SONG

Love still has something of the sea,
    From whence his mother rose;
No time his slaves from doubt can free,
    Nor give their thoughts repose:

They are becalmed in clearest days,
    And in rough weather tost;
They wither under cold delays,
    Or are in tempests lost.

One while they seem to touch the port,
    Then straight into the main,
Some angry wind in cruel sport
    The vessel drives again.

At first disdain and pride they fear,
    Which if they chance to 'scape,
Rivals and falsehood soon appear
    In a more dreadful shape.

By such degrees to Joy they come,
    And are so long withstood,
So slowly they receive the sum,
    It hardly does them good.

'Tis cruel to prolong a pain,
   And to defer a joy,
Believe me, gentle Celemene,
   Offends the wingèd Boy.

An hundred thousand oaths your fears
   Perhaps would not remove;
And if I gazed a thousand years
   I could no deeper love.

SIR CHARLES SEDLEY

32 A SA MAISTRESSE

ODE

  Mignonne, allons voir si la rose
Qui ce matin avoit desclose
Sa robe de pourpre au Soleil,
A point perdu ceste vesprée
Les plis de sa robe pourprée,
Et son teint au vostre pareil.
  Las! voyez comme en peu d'espace,
Mignonne, elle a dessus la place
Las! las! ses beautez laissé cheoir!
O vrayment marastre Nature,
Puis qu'une telle fleur ne dure
Que du matin jusques au soir!
Donc, si vous me croyez, mignonne,
Tandis que vostre âge fleuronne
En sa plus verte nouveauté,
Cueillez, cueillez vostre jeunesse:
Comme à ceste fleur la vieillesse
Fera ternir vostre beauté.

PIERRE DE RONSARD

33 SONG

Go, lovely rose—
Tell her that wastes her time and me,
 That now she knows,
When I resemble her to thee,
How sweet and fair she seems to be.

 Tell her that's young,
And shuns to have her graces spied,
 That hadst thou sprung
In deserts where no men abide,
Thou must have uncommended died.

 Small is the worth
Of beauty from the light retired:
 Bid her come forth,
Suffer herself to be desired,
And not blush so to be admired.

 Then die!—that she
The common fate of all things rare
 May read in thee;
How small a part of time they share
That are so wondrous sweet and fair!

EDMUND WALLER

34

O mistress mine, where are you roaming?
O stay and hear, your true love's coming,
That can sing both high and low.
Trip no further, pretty sweeting.
Journeys end in lover's meeting,
Every wise man's son doth know.

What is love, 'tis not hereafter,
Present mirth, hath present laughter:
What's to come, is still unsure.
In delay there lies no plenty,
Then come kiss me sweet and twenty:
Youth's a stuff will not endure.

WILLIAM SHAKESPEARE

35 TO HIS COY MISTRESS

Had we but world enough, and time,
This coyness, Lady, were no crime.
We would sit down and think which way
To walk and pass our long love's day.
Thou by the Indian Ganges' side
Shouldst rubies find: I by the tide
Of Humber would complain. I would
Love you ten years before the Flood,
And you should, if you please, refuse
Till the conversion of the Jews.
My vegetable love should grow
Vaster than empires, and more slow;
An hundred years should go to praise
Thine eyes and on thy forehead gaze;
Two hundred to adore each breast;
But thirty thousand to the rest;
An age at least to every part,
And the last age should show your heart;
For, Lady, you deserve this state,
Nor would I love at lower rate.
  But at my back I always hear
Time's wingèd chariot hurrying near;

And yonder all before us lie
Deserts of vast eternity.
Thy beauty shall no more be found,
Nor, in thy marble vault, shall sound
My echoing song: then worms shall try
That long preserved virginity,
And your quaint honour turn to dust,
And into ashes all my lust:
The grave's a fine and private place,
But none, I think, do there embrace.
  Now therefore, while the youthful hue
Sits on thy skin like morning dew,
And while thy willing soul transpires
At every pore with instant fires,
Now let us sport us while we may,
And now, like amorous birds of prey,
Rather at once our time devour
Than languish in his slow-chapt power.
Let us roll all our strength and all
Our sweetness up into one ball,
And tear our pleasures with rough strife
Thorough the iron gates of life:
Thus, though we cannot make our sun
Stand still, yet we will make him run.

ANDREW MARVELL

36

Quand vous serez bien vieille, au soir à la chandelle,
Assise aupres du feu, devidant et filant,
Direz chantant mes vers, en vous esmerveillant:
«Ronsard me celebroit du temps que j'estois belle.»

Lors vous n'aurez servante oyant telle nouvelle,
Desja sous le labeur à demy sommeillant,
Qui au bruit de mon nom ne s'aille resveillant,
Benissant vostre nom de louange immortelle.

  Je seray sous la terre, et fantôme sans os
Par les ombres myrteux je prendray mon repos;
Vous serez au fouyer une vieille accroupie,

  Regrettant mon amour et vostre fier desdain.
Vivez, si m'en croyez, n'attendez à demain:
Cueillez dés aujourdhuy les roses de la vie.

PIERRE DE RONSARD

37 [BEAUTY]

Let us use it while we may;
Snatch those joys that haste away.
Earth her winter-coat may cast,
And renew her beauty past;
But, our winter come, in vain
We solicit spring again:
And when our furrows snow shall cover,
Love may return, but never lover.

SIR RICHARD FANSHAWE (from the Italian
of GIOVAN BATTISTA GUARINI)

38 TO THE VIRGINS, TO MAKE MUCH OF TIME

Gather ye rose-buds while ye may,
  Old Time is still a flying:
And this same flower that smiles to-day,
  Tomorrow will be dying.

The glorious lamp of heaven, the Sun,
   The higher he's a getting;
The sooner will his race be run,
   And nearer he's to setting.

That age is best, which is the first,
   When youth and blood are warmer;
But being spent, the worse, and worst
   Times, still succeed the former.

Then be not coy, but use your time;
   And while ye may, go marry:
For having lost but once your prime,
   You may for every tarry.

ROBERT HERRICK

39   BLUE GIRLS

Twirling your blue skirts, travelling the sward
Under the towers of your seminary,
Go listen to your teachers old and contrary
Without believing a word.

Tie the white fillets then about your hair
And think no more of what will come to pass
Than bluebirds that go walking on the grass
And chattering on the air.

Practise your beauty, blue girls, before it fail;
And I will cry with my loud lips and publish
Beauty which all our power shall never establish,
It is so frail.

For I could tell you a story which is true;
I know a lady with a terrible tongue,
Blear eyes fallen from blue,
All her perfections tarnished—yet it is not long
Since she was lovelier than any of you.

JOHN CROWE RANSOM

40

I

Now having leisure, and a happy wind,
Thou mayst at pleasure cause the stones to grind,
Sails spread, and grist here ready to be ground,
Fie, stand not idlely, but let the mill go round.

II

How long shall I pine for love?
　　How long shall I use in vain?
How long like the turtle-dove
　　Shall I heavenly thus complain?
Shall the sails of my love stand still?
　　Shall the grists of my hopes be unground?
Oh fie, oh fie, oh fie,
Let the mill, let the mill go round.

JOHN FLETCHER

When as the rye reach to the chin,
And chopcherry, chopcherry ripe within,
Strawberries swimming in the cream,
And school-boys playing in the stream:
Then O, then O, then O my true love said,
Till that time come again,
She could not live a maid.

GEORGE PEELE

42 INVOCATION QUE LES FILLES POURRONT FAIRE SI ELLES VEULENT SE MARIER

Kyrie, je voudrais,
Christe, être mariée,
Kyrie je prie tous les saints,
Christe que ce soit demain.
Sainte Marie, tout le monde se marie.
Saint Joseph, que vous ai-je fait?
Saint Nicolas, ne m'oubliez pas.
Saint Médéric, que j'aie un bon mari.
Saint Mathieu, qu'il craigne Dieu.
Saint Jean, qu'il m' aime tendrement.
Saint Thibaud, qu'il soit joli et beau.
Saint François, qu'il me soit courtois.
Saint Michel, qu'il me soit fidèle.
Saint André, qu'il soit à mon gré.
Saint Léger, qu'il n'aime pas jouer.
Saint Séverin, qu'il n'aime pas le vin.
Saint Clément, qu'il ait bon coeur.

Saint Nicaise, que je sois à mon aise.
Saint Josse, qu'il me donne un carrosse.
Saint Boniface, que mon marriage se fasse.
Saint Augustin, dès demain matin.

ANON.

43

The maidens came
When I was in my mother's bower,
I had all that I wold.
The bailie beareth the bell away,
The lily, the rose, the rose I lay.

The silver is white,
Red is the gold,
The robes they lay in fold.
The bailie beareth the bell away,
The lily, the rose, the rose I lay.

And through the glass window
Shines the sun.
How should I love and I so young?
The bailie beareth the bell away,
The lily, the rose, the rose I lay.

ANON.

44 [*from* EPITHALAMION]

Wake, now my love, awake; for it is time,
The Rosy Morn long since left Tithon's bed,
All ready to her silver coach to climb,
And Phoebus gins to shew his glorious head.

Hark how the cheerful birds do chaunt their lays
And carol of love's praise.
The merry lark her matins sings aloft,
The thrush replies, the mavis descant plays,
The ouzel shrills, the ruddock warbles soft,
So goodly all agree with sweet consent
To this day's merriment.
Ah my dear love, why do ye sleep thus long,
When meeter were that ye should now awake,
T' await the coming of your joyous make,
And hearken to the birds' love-learnèd song,
The dewy leaves among.
For they of joy and pleasance to you sing,
That all the woods them answer and their echo ring.

My love is now awake out of her dream,
And her fair eyes like stars that dimmèd were
With darksome cloud, now shew their goodly beams
More bright than Hesperus his head doth rear.
Come now ye damsels, daughters of delight,
Help quickly her to dight,
But first come ye, fair hours, which were begot
In love's sweet paradise, of day and night,
Which do the seasons of the year allot,
And all that ever in this world is fair
Do make and still repair.
And ye three handmaids of the Cyprian Queen,
The which do still adorn her beauty's pride,
Help to adorn my beautifullest bride:
And as ye her array, still throw between
Some graces to be seen,
And as ye use to Venus, to her sing,
The whiles the woods shall answer and your echo ring.

Now is my love all ready forth to come,
Let all the virgins therefore well await,

And ye fresh boys that tend upon her groom
Prepare yourselves; for he is coming straight.
Set all your things in seemly good array
Fit for so joyful day,
The joyfulst day that ever sun did see,
Fair Sun, shew forth thy favourable ray,
And let thy lifeful heat not fervent be
For fear of burning her sunshiny face,
Her beauty to disgrace.
O fairest Phoebus, father of the Muse,
If ever I did honour thee aright,
Or sing the thing, that mote thy mind delight,
Do not thy servant's simple boon refuse,
But let this day, let this one day be mine,
Let all the rest be thine.
Then I thy sovereign praises loud will sing,
That all the woods shall answer and their echo ring.

Hark how the minstrels gin to shrill aloud
Their merry music that resounds from far,
The pipe, the tabor, and the trembling crowd,
That well agree withouten breach or jar.
But most of all the damsels do delight,
When they their timbrels smite,
And thereunto do dance and carol sweet,
That all the senses they do ravish quite,
The whiles the boys run up and down the street,
Crying aloud with strong confused noise,
As if it were one voice.
Hymen io Hymen, Hymen they do shout,
That even to the heavens their shouting shrill
Doth reach, and all the firmament doth fill,
To which the people standing all about,
As in approvance do thereto applaud
And loud advance her laud,

And evermore they Hymen Hymen sing,
That all the woods them answer and their echo ring.

*

Ah when will this long weary day have end,
And lend me leave to come unto my love?
How slowly do the hours their numbers spend!
How slowly does sad Time his feathers move!
Haste thee, O fairest Planet, to thy home
Within the western foam:
Thy tired steeds long since have need of rest.
Long though it be, at last I see it gloom,
And the bright evening star with golden crest
Appear out of the east.
Fair child of beauty, glorious lamp of love
That all the host of heaven in ranks dost lead,
And guidest lovers through the nightes dread,
How cheerfully thou lookest from above,
And seemst to laugh atween thy twinkling light
As joying in the sight
Of these glad many which for joy do sing,
That all the woods them answer and their echo ring.

Now cease ye damsels, your delights forepast;
Enough it is, that all the day was yours:
Now day is done, and night is nighing fast:
Now bring the Bride into the bridal bowers.
Now night is come, now soon her disarray,
And in her bed her lay;
Lay her in lilies and in violets,
And silken curtains over her display,
And odour'd sheets, and Arras coverlets.
Behold how goodly my fair love does lie
In proud humility;
Like unto Maia, when as Jove her took,

In Tempe, lying on the flow'ry grass,
Twixt sleep and wake, after she weary was,
With bathing in the Acidalian brook.
Now it is night, ye damsels may be gone,
And leave my love alone,
And leave likewise your former lay to sing:
The woods no more shall answer, nor your echo ring.

Now welcome, Night, thou night so long expected,
That long day's labour dost at last defray,
And all my cares, which cruel love collected,
Hast summed in one, and cancelled for aye:
Spread thy broad wing over my love and me,
That no man may us see,
And in thy sable mantle us enwrap,
From fear of peril and foul horror free.
Let no false treason seek us to entrap,
Nor any dread disquiet once annoy
The safety of our joy:
But let the night be calm and quietsome,
Without tempestuous storms or sad affray:
Like as when Jove with fair Alcmena lay,
When he begat the great Tirynthian groom:
Or like as when he with thy self did lie,
And begot Majesty.
And let the maids and young men cease to sing:
Ne let the woods them answer, nor their echo ring.

EDMUND SPENSER

45

You see the worst of love, but not the best,
Nor will you know him till he comes your guest.
Tho' yearly drops some feather from his sides,
In the heart's temple his pure torch abides.

WALTER SAVAGE LANDOR

46

As you came from the holy land
  Of Walsinghame,
Met you not with my true love
  By the way as you came?

How shall I know your true love,
  That have met many one
As I went to the holy land,
  That have come, that have gone?

She is neither white nor brown,
  But as the heavens fair:
There is none hath a form so divine
  In the earth or the air.

Such a one did I meet, good Sir,
  Such an angelic face,
Who like a queen, like a nymph, did appear,
  By her gait, by her grace.

She hath left me here all alone,
  All alone as unknown,
Who sometimes did me lead with herself,
  And me lov'd as her own.

What's the cause that she leaves you alone
  And a new way doth take,
Who loved you once as her own,
  And her joy did you make?

I have lov'd her all my youth,
  But now old as you see,
Love likes not the falling fruit
  From the withered tree:

Know that Love is a careless child,
  And forgets promise past;
He is blind, he is deaf when he list
  And in faith never fast:

His desire is a dureless content
  And a trustless joy;
He is won with a world of despair
  And is lost with a toy:

Of womenkind such indeed is the love
  Or the word love abused,
Under which many childish desires
  And conceits are excused:

But love is a durable fire,
  In the mind ever burning:
Never sick, never old, never dead,
  From itself never turning.

SIR WALTER RALEGH

47 THE PRIMROSE, BEING AT MONTGOMERY CASTLE, UPON THE HILL, ON WHICH IT IS SITUATE

Upon this Primrose Hill,
  Where, if Heav'n would distill
A shower of rain, each several drop might go
To his own primrose, and grow manna so;
And where their form, and their infinity
  Make a terrestrial galaxy,
  As the small stars do in the sky,
I walk to find a true love; and I see
That 'tis not a mere woman, that is she,
But must, or more, or less than woman be.

Yet know I not which flower
  I wish, a six, or four;
For should my true love less than woman be,
She were scarce any thing; and then, should she
Be more than woman, she would get above
  All thought of sex, and think to move
  My heart to study her, and not to love;
Both these were monsters: since there must reside
Falsehood in woman, I could more abide
She were by art, than nature falsified.

Live, Primrose, then, and thrive
  With thy true number five;
And women, whom this flower doth represent,
With this mysterious number be content;
Ten is the farthest number; if half ten
  Belong unto each woman, then
  Each woman may take half us men;

Or if this will not serve their turn, since all
Numbers are odd or even, and they fall
First into this five, women may take us all.

JOHN DONNE

48 A NOCTURNAL UPON ST LUCY'S DAY, BEING THE SHORTEST DAY

'Tis the year's midnight, and it is the day's,
Lucy's, who scarce seven hours herself unmasks,
    The sun is spent, and now his flasks
    Send forth light squibs, no constant rays;
        The world's whole sap is sunk;
The general balm th' hydroptic earth hath drunk,
Whither, as to the bed's-feet, life is shrunk,
Dead and interr'd; yet all these seem to laugh,
Compar'd with me, who am their epitaph.

Study me then, you who shall lovers be
At the next world, that is, at the next spring:
    For I am every dead thing,
    In whom love wrought new alchemy.
        For his art did express
A quintessence even from nothingness,
From dull privations, and lean emptiness:
He ruin'd me, and I am re-begot
Of absence, darkness, death; things which are not.

All others, from all things, draw all that's good,
Life, soul, form, spirit, whence they being have;
    I, by love's limbeck, am the grave
    Of all, that's nothing. Oft a flood
        Have we two wept, and so

Drown'd the whole world, us two; oft did we grow
To be two chaoses, when we did show
Care to ought else; and often absences
Withdrew our souls, and made us carcasses.

But I am by her death, (which word wrongs her)
Of the first nothing, the elixir grown;
   Were I a man, that I were one,
  I needs must know; I should prefer,
    If I were any beast,
Some ends, some means; yea plants, yea stones detest
And love; all, all some properties invest;
If I an ordinary nothing were,
As shadow, a light, and body must be here.

But I am none; nor will my sun renew.
You lovers, for whose sake the lesser sun
   At this time to the Goat is run
  To fetch new lust, and give it you,
    Enjoy your summer all;
Since she enjoys her long night's festival,
Let me prepare towards her, and let me call
This hour her vigil, and her eve, since this
Both the year's, and the day's deep midnight is.

JOHN DONNE

49 MARRIAGE MORNING

Light, so low upon earth,
   You send a flash to the sun.
Here is the golden close of love,
   All my wooing is done.

Oh, the woods and the meadows,
  Woods where we hid from the wet,
Stiles where we stay'd to be kind,
  Meadows in which we met!

Light, so low in the vale
  You flash and lighten afar,
For this is the golden morning of love,
  And you are his morning star.
Flash, I am coming, I come,
  By meadow and stile and wood,
Oh, lighten into my eyes and heart,
  Into my heart and my blood!

Heart, are you great enough
  For a love that never tires?
O heart, are you great enough for love?
  I have heard of thorns and briers.
Over the thorns and briers,
  Over the meadows and stiles,
Over the world to the end of it
  Flash for a million miles.

ALFRED TENNYSON

50

Across the sky the daylight crept,
  And birds grew garrulous in the grove,
And on my marriage-morn I slept
  A soft sleep, undisturb'd by love.

COVENTRY PATMORE

I thought once how Theocritus had sung
Of the sweet years, the dear and wished-for years,
Who each one in a gracious hand appears
To bear a gift for mortals, old or young:
And, as I mused it in his antique tongue,
I saw, in gradual vision through my tears,
The sweet, sad years, the melancholy years, . . .
Those of my own life, who by turns had flung
A shadow across me. Straightway I was 'ware,
So weeping, how a mystic Shape did move
Behind me, and drew me backward by the hair;
And a voice said in mastery while I strove, . . .
'Guess now who holds thee?'—'Death,' I said. But, there,
The silver answer rang, . . . 'Not Death, but Love.'

ELIZABETH BARRETT BROWNING

52   [LOVE PURSUED]

Art thou gone in haste?
    I'll not forsake thee;
Runn'st thou ne'er so fast,
    I'll o'ertake thee:
O'er the dales, o'er the downs,
    Through the green meadows,
From the fields through the towns,
    To the dim shadows.

All along the plains,
    To the low fountains,
Up and down agen
    From the high mountains;

Echo then, shall agen
   Tell her I follow,
And the floods to the woods
   Carry my holla, holla, *ce,la,ho,ho,hu.*

ANON.

53 LOVERS HOW THEY COME AND PART

A Gyges Ring they bear about them still,
To be, and not seen when and where they will.
They tread on clouds, and though they sometimes fall,
They fall like dew, but make no noise at all.
So silently they one to th'other come,
As colours steal into the pear or plum,
And air-like, leave no pression to be seen
Where'er they met, or parting place has been.

ROBERT HERRICK

54

O friends! who have accompanied thus far
My quickening steps, sometimes where sorrow sate
Dejected, and sometimes where valour stood
Resplendent, right before us; here perhaps
We best might part; but one to valour dear
Comes up in wrath and calls me worse than foe,
Reminding me of gifts too ill deserved.
I must not blow away the flowers he gave,
Altho' now faded; I must not efface
The letters his own hand has traced for me.
   Here terminates my park of poetry.

Look out no longer for extensive woods,
For clusters of unlopt and lofty trees,
With stately animals coucht under them,
Or grottoes with deep wells of water pure,
And ancient figures in the solid rock:
Come, with our sunny pasture be content,
Our narrow garden and our homestead croft,
And tillage not neglected. Love breathes round;
Love, the bright atmosphere, the vital air,
Of youth; without it life and death are one.

WALTER SAVAGE LANDOR

55 [from LOVE'S LABOUR'S LOST]

(Berowne speaks)

A lover's eyes will gaze an eagle blind,
A lover's ear will hear the lowest sound,
When the suspicious head of theft is stopped.
Love's feeling is more soft and sensible
Than are the tender horns of cockled snails.
Love's tongue proves dainty Bacchus gross in taste.
For valour, is not Love a Hercules,
Still climbing trees in the Hesperides?
Subtle as Sphinx; as sweet and musical
As bright Apollo's lute, strung with his hair.
And when Love speaks, the voice of all the gods
Makes heaven drowsy with the harmony.
Never durst poet touch a pen to write
Until his ink were temp'red with Love's sighs;
O then his lines would ravish savage ears
And plant in tyrants mild humility,

From women's eyes this doctrine I derive.
They sparkle still the right Promethean fire;
They are the books, the arts, the academes,
That show, contain, and nourish all the world.

WILLIAM SHAKESPEARE

56 [*from* THE WINTER'S TALE]

PERDITA Here's flowers for you,
Hot lavender, mints, savory, marjoram,
The marigold, that goes to bed wi' th' sun
And with him rises weeping. These are flowers
Of middle summer, and I think they are given
To men of middle age. Y'are very welcome.

CAMILLO
I should leave grazing, were I of your flock,
And only live by gazing.

PERDITA Out, alas!
You'd be so lean that blasts of January
Would blow you through and through. Now, my fair'st friend,
I would I had some flowers o' th' spring that might
Become your time of day, and yours, and yours,
That wear upon your virgin branches yet
Your maidenheads growing. O Proserpina,
For the flowers now that, frighted, thou let'st fall
From Dis's wagon; daffodils,
That come before the swallow dares, and take
The winds of March with beauty; violets dim,
But sweeter than the lids of Juno's eyes
Or Cytherea's breath; pale primroses,
That die unmarried, ere they can behold

Bright Phoebus in his strength—a malady
Most incident to maids; bold oxlips and
The crown imperial; lilies of all kinds,
The flower-de-luce being one. O, these I lack
To make you garlands of, and my sweet friend,
To strew him o'er and o'er!

FLORIZEL   What, like a corse?

PERDITA

No, like a bank for love to lie and play on.
Not like a corse, or if, not to be buried,
But quick and in mine arms. Come, take your flowers.
Methinks I play as I have seen them do
In Whitsun pastorals. Sure this robe of mine
Does change my disposition.

FLORIZEL   What you do
Still betters what is done. When you speak, sweet,
I'd have you do it ever. When you sing,
I'd have you buy and sell so, so give alms,
Pray so, and for the ord'ring your affairs,
To sing them too. When you do dance, I wish you
A wave o' th' sea, that you might ever do
Nothing but that, move still, still so,
And own no other function. Each your doing,
So singular in each particular,
Crowns what you are doing in the present deeds,
That all your acts are queens.

PERDITA   O Doricles,
Your praises are too large. But that your youth,
And the true blood which peeps fairly through 't,
Do plainly give you out an unstained shepherd,
With wisdom I might fear, my Doricles,
You wooed me the false way.

FLORIZEL   I think you have
As little skill to fear as I have purpose
To put you to 't. But come; our dance, I pray.

Your hand, my Perdita. So turtles pair
That never mean to part.

WILLIAM SHAKESPEARE

57

Blest, blest and happy he
Whose eyes behold her face,
But blessed more whose ears hath heard
The speeches framed with grace.

And he is half a god
That these thy lips may kiss,
Yet god all whole that may enjoy
    Thy body as it is.

ANON.

58   SONG FOR AUTUMN

Come, love, for now the night and day
    Play with their pawns of black and white,
And what day loses in her play
    Is won by the encroaching night.

The clematis grows old and clings
    Grey-bearded to the road-side trees
And in the hedge the nightshade strings
    Her berries in bright necklaces.

The fields are bare; the latest sheaf
    Of barley, wheat and rusty rye
Is stacked long since; and every leaf
    Burns like a sunset on the sky.

Come, love, for night and day, alas,
  Are playing for a heavier stake
Than hours of light or leaves or grass;
  Come, love; come, love, for sweet love's sake.

ANDREW YOUNG

2

LOVE BEGUN

What fair pomp have I spied of glittering Ladies,
With locks sparkled abroad, and rosy coronet
On their ivory brows, track'd to the dainty thighs
With robes like Amazons, blue as violet,
With gold aglets adorn'd, some in a changeable
Pale, with spangs wavering, taught to be moveable.

Then those Knights that afar off with a dolorous viewing
Cast their eyes hitherward: lo, in an agony,
All unbrac'd, cry aloud, their heavy state rueing:
Moist cheeks with blubbering, painted as ebony
Black; their felter'd hair torn with wrathful hand:
And whiles astonied, stark in a maze they stand.

But hark, what merry sound! what sudden harmony!
Look, look near the grove where the Ladies do tread
With their Knights the measures weigh'd by the melody!
Wantons, whose travesing make men enamoured!
Now they fain an honour, now by the slender waist
He must lift her aloft, and seal a kiss in haste.

Straight down under a shadow for weariness they lie
With pleasant daliance, hand knit with arm in arm;
Now close, now set aloof, they gaze with an equal eye,
Changing kisses alike; straight with a false alarm,
Mocking kisses alike, pout with a lovely lip.
Thus drown'd with jollities, their merry days do slip.

But stay! now I discern they go on a pilgrimage
Toward Love's holy land, fair Paphos or Cyprus.

Such devotion is meet for a blithsome age;
With sweet youth it agrees well to be amorous.
Let old angry fathers lurk in an hermitage:
Come, we'll associate this jolly pilgrimage!

THOMAS CAMPION

60 LES GERTRUDE HOFFMANN GIRLS

Gertrude, Dorothy, Mary, Claire, Alberta,
Charlotte, Dorothy, Ruth, Catherine, Emma,
Louise, Margaret, Ferral, Harriet, Sara,
Florence toute nue, Margaret, Toots, Thelma,

Belles-de-nuits, belles-de-feu, belles-de-pluie,
Le cœur tremblant, les mains cachées, les yeux au vent,
Vous me montrez les mouvements de la lumière,
Vous échangez un regard clair pour un printemps,

Le tour de votre taille pour un tour de fleur,
L'audace et le danger pour votre chair sans ombre,
Vous échangez l'amour pour des frissons d'épées,
Des rires inconscients pour des promesses d'aube.

Vos danses sont le gouffre effrayant de mes songes
Et je tombe et ma chute éternise ma vie,
L'espace sous vos pieds est de plus en plus vaste,
Merveilles, vous dansez sur les sources du ciel.

PAUL ELUARD

61 AMO, AMAS

Amo, Amas, I love a lass
As a cedar tall and slender;
Sweet cowslip's grace is her nominative case,
And she's of the feminine gender.

    Rorum, Corum, sunt divorum,
    Harum, Scarum divo;
    Tag-rag, merry-derry, periwig and hat-band
    Hic hoc horum genitivo.

Can I decline a Nymph divine?
Her voice as a flute is dulcis.
Her oculus bright, her manus white,
And soft, when I tacto, her pulse is.

    Rorum, Corum, sunt divorum,
    Harum, Scarum divo;
    Tag-rag, merry-derry, periwig and hat-band
    Hic hoc horum genitivo.

Oh, how bella my puella,
I'll kiss secula seculorum.
If I've luck, sir, she's my uxor,
O dies benedictorum.

    Rorum, Corum, sunt divorum,
    Harum, Scarum divo;
    Tag-rag, merry-derry, periwig and hat-band
    Hic hoc horum genitivo.

JOHN O'KEEFE

62

Only joy, now here you are,
Fit to hear and ease my care;
Let my whispering voice obtain
Sweet reward for sharpest pain;
Take me to thee, and thee to me.
No, no, no, no, my dear, let be.

Night hath closed all in her cloak,
Twinkling stars love-thoughts provoke,
Danger hence good care doth keep,
Jealousy itself doth sleep;
Take me to thee, and thee to me.
No, no, no, no, my dear, let be.

Better place no wit can find,
Cupid's yoke to loose or bind;
These sweet flowers on fine bed too
Us in their best language woo;
Take me to thee, and thee to me.
No, no, no, no, my dear, let be.

This small light the moon bestows
Serves thy beams but to disclose;
So to raise my hap more high,
Fear not, else none can us spy;
Take me to thee, and thee to me.
No, no, no, no, my dear, let be.

That you heard was but a mouse,
Dumb sleep holdeth all the house;
Yet asleep, methinks, they say,
Young folks, take time while you may;
Take me to thee, and thee to me.
No, no, no, no, my dear, let be.

Niggard Time threats, if we miss
This large offer of our bliss,
Long stay ere he grant the same;
Sweet, then, while each thing doth frame,
Take me to thee, and thee to me.
No, no, no, no, my dear, let be.

Your fair mother is a-bed,
Candles out and curtains spread;
She thinks you do letters write;
Write, but let me first indite;
Take me to thee, and thee to me.
No, no, no, no, my dear, let be.

Sweet, alas, why strive you thus?
Concord better fitteth us;
Leave to Mars the force of hands,
Your power in your beauty stands;
Take thee to me, and me to thee.
No, no, no, no, my dear, let be.

Woe to me, and do you swear
Me to hate? but I forbear;
Cursed be my destines all,
That brought me so high to fall;
Soon with my death I will please thee.
No, no, no, no, my dear, let be.

SIR PHILIP SIDNEY

63 [*from* THE TWO GENTLEMEN OF VERONA]

(*Proteus speaks*)

Thus have I shunned the fire for fear of burning,
And drenched me in the sea, where I am drowned.
I feared to show my father Julia's letter,
Lest he should take exceptions to my love;
And with the vantage of mine own excuse
Hath he excepted most against my love.
O, how this spring of love resembleth
The uncertain glory of an April day,
Which now shows all the beauty of the sun,
And by and by a cloud takes all away!

WILLIAM SHAKESPEARE

64

I can not tell, not I, why she
Awhile so gracious, now should be
So grave: I can not tell you why
The violet hangs its head awry.
It shall be cull'd, it shall be worn,
In spite of every sign of scorn,
Dark look, and overhanging thorn.

WALTER SAVAGE LANDOR

65 [SAMELA]

Like to Diana in her summer weed
Girt with a crimson robe of brightest die,
goes fair Samela.

Whiter than be the flocks that straggling feed,
When washed by Arethusa, faint they lie,
   is fair Samela.
As fair Aurora in her morning gray
Deck'd with the ruddy glister of her love,
   is fair Samela.
Like lovely Thetis on a calmed day,
When as her brightness Neptune's fancy move,
   shines fair Samela.
Her tresses gold, her eyes like glassy streams,
Her teeth are pearls, the breast of ivory
   of fair Samela.
Her cheeks like rose and lily yield forth gleams,
Her brows' bright arches fram'd of ebony:
   thus fair Samela.
Passeth fair Venus in her bravest hue,
And Juno in the show of majesty,
   for she's Samela.
Pallas in wit, all three if you will view,
For beauty, wit and matchless dignity
   yield to Samela.

ROBERT GREENE

66

Crabbed age and youth cannot live together:
Youth is full of pleasance, age is full of care;
Youth like summer morn, age like winter weather;
Youth like summer brave, age like winter bare.
Youth is full of sport, age's breath is short;
Youth is nimble, age is lame;
Youth is hot and bold, age is weak and cold;
Youth is wild, and age is tame.

Age, I do abhor thee; youth, I do adore thee.
O, my love, my love is young!
Age, I do defy thee. O sweet shepherd, hie thee,
For methinks thou stays too long.

WILLIAM SHAKESPEARE

67 WHITE AN' BLUE

My love is o' comely height, an' straight,
An' comely in all her ways an' gait,
In feäce she do show the rwose's hue,
An' her lids on her eyes be white on blue.

When Elemley clubmen walk'd in Maÿ
An' vo'k come in clusters, ev'ry waÿ,
As soon as the zun dried up the dew,
An' clouds in the sky wer white on blue,

She come by the down, wi' trippen walk,
By deäisies, an' sheenen banks o' chalk,
An' brooks, where the crowvoot flow'rs did strew
The sky-tinted water, white on blue.

She nodded her head, as plaÿ'd the band;
She dapp'd wi' her voot, as she did stand;
She danced in a reel, a-wearen new
A skirt wi' a jacket, white wi' blue.

I singled her out vrom thin an' stout,
Vrom slender an' stout I chose her out;
An' what, in the evenen, could I do,
But gi'e her my breast-knot, white an' blue?

WILLIAM BARNES

68 HEXAMETRA ALEXIS IN LAUDEM
ROSAMUNDI

Oft have I heard my lief Corydon report on a love-day,
When bonny maids do meet with the swains in the valley by Tempe,
How bright eyed his Phyllis was, how lovely they glanced,
When fro th'arches ebon black, flew looks as a lightning,
That set afire with piercing flames even hearts adamantine:
Face rose hued, cherry red, with a silver taint like a lily.
Venus' pride might abate, might abash with a blush to behold her.
Phoebus' wires compar'd to her hairs unworthy the praising.
Juno's state, and Pallas' wit disgrac'd with the Graces,
That grac'd her, whom poor Corydon did choose for a love-mate:
Ah, but had Corydon now seen the star that Alexis
Likes and loves so dear, that he melts to sighs when he sees her.
Did Corydon but see those eyes, those amorous eyelids,
From whence fly holy flames of death or life in a moment.
Ah, did he see that face, those hairs that Venus, Apollo
Basht to behold, and both disgrac'd, did grieve, that a creature
Should exceed in hue, compare both a god and a goddess:
Ah, had he seen my sweet paramour, the saint of Alexis,
Then had he said, Phyllis, sit down surpassed in all points,
For there is one more fair than thou, beloved of Alexis.

ROBERT GREENE

69 TAM I' THE KIRK

O Jean, my Jean, when the bell ca's the congregation
Owre valley an' hill wi' the ding frae its iron mou,
When a'body's thochts is set on his ain salvation,
    Mine's set on you.

There's a reid rose lies on the Buik o' the Word afore ye
That was growin' braw on its bush at the keek o' day,
But the lad that pu'd yon flower i' the mornin's glory,
      He canna pray.

He canna pray; but there's nane i' the kirk will heed him
Whaur he sits sae still his lane at the side o' the wa'
For nane but the reid rose kens what my lassie gie'd him—
      It an' us twa!

He canna sing for the sang that his ain he'rt raises,
He canna see for the mist that's afore his een,
And a voice drouns the hale o' the psalms an' the paraphrases,
      Cryin' 'Jean, Jean, Jean!'

VIOLET JACOB

70 [from SAPPHO]

Mother, I cannot mind my wheel;
   My fingers ache, my lips are dry:
Oh! if you felt the pain I feel!
   But Oh, who ever felt as I?

No longer could I doubt him true;
   All other men may use deceit:
He always said my eyes were blue,
   And often swore my lips were sweet.

WALTER SAVAGE LANDOR

71 QUEENS

Seven dog-days we let pass
Naming Queens in Glenmacnass,
All the rare and royal names
Wormy sheepskin yet retains,
Etain, Helen, Maeve, and Fand,
Golden Deirdre's tender hand,
Bert, the big-foot, sung by Villon,
Cassandra, Ronsard found in Lyon.
Queens of Sheba, Meath and Connaught,
Coifed with crown, or gaudy bonnet,
Queens whose finger once did stir men,
Queens were eaten of fleas and vermin,
Queens men drew like Monna Lisa,
Or slew with drugs in Rome and Pisa,
We named Lucrezia Crivelli,
And Titian's lady with amber belly,
Queens acquainted in learned sin,
Jane of Jewry's slender shin:
Queens who cut the bogs of Glanna,
Judith of Scripture, and Gloriana,
Queens who wasted the East by proxy,
Or drove the ass-cart, a tinker's doxy,
Yet these are rotten—I ask their pardon—
And we've the sun on rock and garden,
These are rotten, so you're the Queen
Of all are living, or have been.

J. M. SYNGE

72 ON A BIRTHDAY

Friend of Ronsard, Nashe, and Beaumont,
Lark of Ulster, Meath and Thomond,
Heard from Smyrna and Sahara
To the surf of Connemara,
Lark of April, June, and May,
Sing loudly this my Lady-day.

J. M. SYNGE

73 TO THE LADY MAY

Your smiles are not, as other women's be,
Only the drawing of the mouth awry;
For breasts and cheeks and forehead we may see,
Parts wanting motion, all stand smiling by.
Heaven hath no mouth, and yet is said to smile
            After your style;
No more hath Earth, yet that smiles too,
            Just as you do.

No simpering lips nor looks can breed
Such smiles as from your face proceed.
The sun must lend his golden beams,
   Soft winds their breath, green trees their shade,
Sweet fields their flowers, clear springs their streams,
   Ere such another smile be made.
But these concurring, we may say,
So smiles the spring, and so smiles lovely May.

AURELIAN TOWNSEND

74

Je plante en ta faveur cest arbre de Cybelle,
Ce pin, où tes honneurs se liront tous les jours:
J'ay gravé sur le tronc nos noms et nos amours,
Qui croistront à l'envy de l'escorce nouvelle.

Faunes qui habitez ma terre paternelle,
Qui menez sur le Loir vos dances et vos tours,
Favorisez la plante et luy donnez secours,
Que l'Esté ne la brusle, et l'Hyver ne la gelle.

Pasteur, qui conduiras en ce lieu ton troupeau,
Flageolant une Eclogue en ton tuyau d'aveine,
Attache tous les ans à cest arbre un tableau,

Qui tesmoigne aux passans mes amours et ma peine;
Puis l'arrosant de laict et du sang d'un agneau,
Dy: «Ce pin est sacré, c'est la plante d'Helene.»

PIERRE DE RONSARD

75 SPECTRAL LOVERS

By night they haunted a thicket of April mist,
Out of that black ground suddenly come to birth,
Else angels lost in each other and fallen on earth.
Lovers they knew they were, but why unclasped, unkissed?
Why should two lovers be frozen apart in fear?
And yet they were, they were.

Over the shredding of an April blossom
Scarcely her fingers touched him, quick with care,
Yet of evasions even she made a snare.
The heart was bold that clanged within her bosom,
The moment perfect, the time stopped for them,
Still her face turned from him.

Strong were the batteries of the April night
And the stealthy emanations of the field;
Should the walls of her prison undefended yield
And open her treasure to the first clamorous knight?
'This is the mad moon, and shall I surrender all?
If he but ask it I shall.'

And gesturing largely to the moon of Easter,
Mincing his steps and swishing the jubilant grass,
Beheading some field-flowers that had come to pass,
He had reduced his tributaries faster
Had not considerations pinched his heart
Unfitly for his art.

'Do I reel with the sap of April like a drunkard?
Blessed is he that taketh this richest of cities;
But it is so stainless the sack were a thousand pities.
This is that marble fortress not to be conquered,
Lest its white peace in the black flame turn to tinder
And an unutterable cinder.'

They passed me once in April, in the mist.
No other season is it when one walks and discovers
Two tall and wandering, like spectral lovers,
White in the season's moon-gold and amethyst,
Who touch quick fingers fluttering like a bird
Whose songs shall never be heard.

JOHN CROWE RANSOM

76 FIRST LOVE

I ne'er was struck before that hour
   With love so sudden and so sweet,
Her face it bloomed like a sweet flower
   And stole my heart away complete.

My face turned pale as deadly pale,
  My legs refused to walk away,
And when she looked, what could I ail?
  My life and all seemed turned to clay.

And then my blood rushed to my face
  And took my eyesight quite away,
The trees and bushes round the place
  Seemed midnight at noonday.
I could not see a single thing,
  Words from my eyes did start—
They spoke as chords do from the string,
  And blood burnt round my heart.

Are flowers the winter's choice?
  Is love's bed always snow?
She seemed to hear my silent voice,
  Not love's appeals to know.
I never saw so sweet a face
  As that I stood before.
My heart has left its dwelling-place
  And can return no more.

JOHN CLARE

77 THE SECRET

I loved thee, though I told thee not,
  Right earlily and long,
Thou wert my joy in every spot,
  My theme in every song.

And when I saw a stranger face
  Where beauty held the claim,
I gave it like a secret grace
  The being of thy name.

And all the charms of face or voice
   Which I in others see
Are but the recollected choice
   Of what I felt for thee.

JOHN CLARE

78 SONG

The lark now leaves his wat'ry nest,
   And climbing, shakes his dewy wings;
He takes this window for the east,
   And to implore your light, he sings,
Awake, awake, the morn will never rise,
Till she can dress her beauty at your eyes.

The merchant bows unto the seaman's star,
   The ploughman from the sun his season takes;
But still the lover wonders what they are,
   Who look for day before his mistress wakes.
Awake, awake, break through your veils of lawn,
Then draw your curtains, and begin the dawn.

SIR JOHN DAVENANT

79 SONG: TO CELIA

Drink to me, only, with thine eyes,
   And I will pledge with mine;
Or leave a kiss but in the cup,
   And I'll not look for wine.

The thirst, that from the soul doth rise,
    Doth ask a drink divine:
But might I of Jove's nectar sup,
    I would not change for thine.
I sent thee, late, a rosy wreath,
    Not so much honouring thee,
As giving it a hope, that there
    It could not withered be.
But thou thereon did'st only breath,
    And sent'st it back to me:
Since when it grows, and smells, I swear,
    Not of itself, but thee.

BEN JONSON

80

Pack, clouds, away, and welcome, day!
With night we banish sorrow;
Sweet air, blow soft; mount, lark, aloft
To give my love good-morrow.
Wings from the wind, to please her mind,
Notes from the lark I'll borrow:
Bird, prune thy wing; nightingale, sing,
To give my love good-morrow.
To give my love good-morrow
Notes from them all I'll borrow.

Wake from thy nest, robin red-breast!
Sing, birds, in every furrow;
And from each bill let music shrill
Give my fair love good-morrow.
Blackbird and thrush, in every bush,
Stare, linnet and cocksparrow,

You pretty elves, among yourselves,
Sing my fair love good-morrow.
To give my love good-morrow
Sing, birds in every furrow.

THOMAS HEYWOOD

81

My ghostly fadir I me confess
First to God and then to you
That at a window wot ye how
I stale a cosse of great sweetness
Which done was out avisiness,
But it is done not undone now,
  My ghostly fadir I me confess
  First to God and then to you.
But I restore it shall doubtless
Again if so be that I mow
And that to God I make a vow
And elles I axe foryefnes.
  My ghostly fadir I me confess
  First to God and then to you.

CHARLES D'ORLÉANS

82

Fair Phyllis I saw sitting all alone,
  Feeding her flock near to the mountain side.
The shepherds knew not whither she was gone,
  But after, her love Amyntas hied.

Up and down he wandered whilst she was missing;
When he found her, O then they fell a-kissing.

ANON.

83 A THUNDERSTORM IN TOWN

She wore a new 'terra-cotta' dress,
And we stayed, because of the pelting storm,
Within the hansom's dry recess,
Though the horse had stopped; yea, motionless
   We sat on, snug and warm.

Then the downpour ceased, to my sharp sad pain
And the glass that had screened our forms before
Flew up, and out she sprang to her door:
I should have kissed her if the rain
   Had lasted a minute more.

THOMAS HARDY

84

Thyrsis and Milla, arm in arm together,
In merry May to the green garden walked,
Where all the way they wanton riddles talked,
The youthful boy, kissing her cheeks all rosy,
Beseech'd her there to gather him a posy.

She straight her light green silken coats up tucked
And may for Mill and thyme for Thyrsis plucked,
Which when she brought he clasp'd her by the middle,
And kiss'd her sweet but could not read her riddle,
Ah fool, with that the Nymph set up a laughter,
And blush'd, and ran away, and he ran after.

ANON.

85 RONDEAU

Blanche com lis, plus que rose vermeille,
Resplendissant com rubis d'Oriant,

En remirant vo biauté nonpareille,
Blanche com lis, plus que rose vermeille,

Sui si ravis que mes cuers toudis veille
Afin que serve a loy de fin amant,
Blanche com lys, plus que rose vermeille,
Resplendissant com rubis d'Oriant.

GUILLAUME DE MACHAUT

86 IANTHE'S TROUBLES

From you, Ianthe, little troubles pass
    Like little ripples down a sunny river;
Your pleasures spring like daisies in the grass,
    Cut down, and up again as blithe as ever.

WALTER SAVAGE LANDOR

87

Thou hast not rais'd, Ianthe, such desire
    In any breast as thou hast rais'd in mine.
No wandering meteor now, no marshy fire,
    Leads on my steps, but lofty, but divine:

And, if thou chillest me, as chill thou dost
   When I approach too near, too boldly gaze,
So chills the blushing morn, so chills the host
   Of vernal stars, with light more chaste than day's.

WALTER SAVAGE LANDOR

88

Within a greenwood sweet of myrtle savour,
Whenas the earth was with fair flowers revested,
I saw a shepherd with his nymph that rested.
Thus spake the nymph with sugared words of favour:
Say (sweet love) to thy love, tell me, my darling,
Where is thy heart bestowed? Where is thy liking?
The shepherd answered then with a deep sighing,
All full of sweetness and of sorrow mixed:
On thee, dainty dear life, my love is fixed.
With that the gentle nymph, full sweetly smiling,
With kind words of delight and flattering glozes,
She kindly kissed his cheek with lips of roses.

ANON. (from the Italian)

89

Or, nous cueillions ensemble la pervenche.

   Je soupirais, je crois qu'elle rêvait.
   Ma joue à peine avait un blond duvet.
   Elle avait mis son jupon du dimanche;
   Je le baissais chaque fois qu'une branche
           Le relevait.

Et nous cueillions ensemble la pervenche.

Le diable est fin, mais nous sommes bien sots.
Elle s'assit sous de charmants berceaux
Près d'un ruisseau qui dans l'herbe s'épanche;
Et vous chantiez dans votre gaîté franche,
          Petits oiseaux.

Et nous cueillions ensemble la pervenche.

Le paradis pourtant m'était échu.
En ce moment, un bouc au pied fourchu
Passe et me dit: Penche-toi. Je me penche.
Anges du ciel! je vis sa gorge blanche
          Sous son fichu!

Et nous cueillions ensemble la pervenche.

J'étais bien jeune et j'avais peur d'oser.
Elle me dit: Viens donc te reposer
Sous mon ombrelle, et me donna du manche
Un petit coup, et je pris ma revanche
          Par un baiser.

Et nous cueillions ensemble la pervenche.

VICTOR HUGO

90 A RED, RED ROSE

O my Luve's like a red, red rose,
  That's newly sprung in June;
O my Luve's like the melodie
  That's sweetly play'd in tune.—

As fair art thou, my bonie lass,
   So deep in luve am I;
And I will love thee still, my Dear,
   Till a' the seas gang dry.—

Till a' the seas gang dry, my Dear,
   And the rocks melt wi' the sun:
I will love thee still, my Dear,
   While the sands o' life shall run.—

And fare thee weel, my only Luve!
   And fare thee weel, a while!
And I will come again, my Luve,
   Tho' it were ten thousand mile!

ROBERT BURNS

91 A UNE FEMME

Enfant! si j'étais roi, je donnerais l'empire,
Et mon char, et mon sceptre, et mon peuple à genoux,
Et ma couronne d'or, et mes bains de porphyre,
Et mes flottes, à qui la mer ne peut suffire,
      Pour un regard de vous!

Si j'étais Dieu, la terre et l'air avec les ondes,
Les anges, les démons courbés devant ma loi,
Et le profond chaos aux entrailles fécondes,
L'éternité, l'espace, et les cieux, et les mondes,
      Pour un baiser de toi!

VICTOR HUGO

92 O WERE MY LOVE YON LILAC FAIR

O were my Love yon lilack fair,
　Wi' purple blossoms to the spring;
And I, a bird to shelter there,
　When wearied on my little wing.

How I wad mourn, when it was torn
　By autumn wild, and winter rude!
But I wad sing on wanton wing,
　When youthfu' May its bloom renew'd.

O gin my love were yon red rose,
　That grows upon the castle wa'!
And I mysel' a drap o' dew,
　Into her bonnie breast to fa'!

Oh, there beyond expression blest
　I'd feast on beauty a' the night;
Seal'd on her silk-saft faulds to rest,
　Till fley'd awa by Phebus' light!

ROBERT BURNS

93 [from PARADISE LOST]

(*Eve speaks to Adam*)

　With thee conversing I forget all time,
　All seasons and their change, all please alike.
　Sweet is the breath of morn, her rising sweet,
　With charm of earliest birds; pleasant the sun
　When first on this delightful land he spreads
　His orient beams, on herb, tree, fruit, and flower,

Glistring with dew; fragrant the fertile earth
After soft showers; and sweet the coming on
Of grateful evening mild, then silent night
With this her solemn bird and this fair moon,
And these the gems of heav'n, her starry train:
But neither breath of morn when she ascends
With charm of earliest birds, nor rising sun
On this delightful land, nor herb, fruit, flower,
Glistring with dew, nor fragrance after showers,
Nor grateful evening mild, nor silent night
With this her solemn bird, nor walk by moon,
Or glittering starlight without thee is sweet.

JOHN MILTON

94 MADRIGAL

Like the Idalian queen
Her hair about her eyne,
With neck and breasts' ripe apples to be seen,
At the first glance of the morn
In Cyprus gardens gathering those fair flowers
Which of her blood were born,
I saw, but fainting saw, my paramours.
The Graces naked danc'd about the place,
The winds and trees amaz'd
With silence on her gaz'd,
The flow'rs did smile, like those upon her face,
And as their aspen stalks those fingers band,
(That she might read my case)
A hyacinth I wish'd me in her hand.

WILLIAM DRUMMOND OF HAWTHORNDEN

Her face   Her tongue   Her wit
so fair   so sweet   so sharp
first bent   then drew   then hit
mine eye   mine ear   my heart

Mine eye   Mine ear   My heart
to like   to learn   to love
her face   her tongue   her wit
doth lead   doth teach   doth move

Her face   Her tongue   Her wit
with beams   with sound   with art
doth blind   doth charm   doth knit
mine eye   mine ear   my heart

Mine eye   Mine ear   My heart
with life   with hope   with skill
her face   her tongue   her wit
doth feed   doth feast   doth fill

O face   O tongue   O wit
with frowns   with checks   with smart
wrong not   vex not   wound not
mine eye   mine ear   my heart

This eye   This ear   This heart
shall joy   shall yield   shall swear
her face   her tongue   her wit
to serve   to trust   to fear.

SIR ARTHUR GORGES

En vain l'aurore,
Qui se colore,
Annonce un jour
Fait pour l'amour;
De ta pensée
Tout oppressée,
Pour te revoir,
J'attends le soir.

L'aurore, en fuite,
Laisse à sa suite
Un soleil pur,
Un ciel d'azur;
L'amour s'éveille;
Pour lui je veille;
Et, pour te voir,
J'attends le soir.

Heure charmante,
Soyez moins lente!
Avancez-vous,
Moment si doux!
Une journée
Est une année,
Quand, pour te voir,
J'attends le soir.

Un voile sombre
Ramène l'ombre;
Un doux repos
Suit les travaux:

Mon sein palpite,
Mon cœur me quitte . . .
Je vais te voir;
Voilà le soir.

MARCELINE DESBORDES-VALMORE

97

Henceforth I will not set my love
　On other than the country lass,
For in the court I see and prove
　Fancy is brittle as the glass.
The love bestowed on the great
　Is ever full of toil and cares,
Subject still to frown and freat,
　With sugar'd baits in subtle snares.
In good old times it was the guise
　To show things in their proper kind,
Love painted out in naked wise
　To show his plain and single mind.
But since into the court he came
　Infected with a braver style
He lost both property and name,
　Attired all in craft and guile.
Yet in the village still he keeps,
　And merry makes with little cost,
But never breaks their quiet sleeps
　With jealous thoughts or labour lost.
What though in silver and in gold
　The bonny lass be not so brave
Yet are her looks fresh to behold
　And that is it that love doth crave.

Fair fall the petticoat of red
   That veils the skin as white as milk,
And such as would not so be sped
   Let them go coy the gowns of silk.
Keep, ladies, keep for your own turns
   The Spanish red to mend your looks,
For when the sun my Daphne burns
   She seeks the water of the brooks,
And though the musk and amber fine
   So ladylike she cannot get,
Yet will she wear the sweet woodbine,
   The primrose and the violet.

SIR ARTHUR GORGES

98

Still to be neat, still to be drest,
As you were going to a feast;
Still to be powder'd, still perfum'd:
Lady, it is to be presum'd,
Though art's hid causes are not found,
All is not sweet, all is not sound.

Give me a look, give me a face,
That makes simplicity a grace;
Robes loosely flowing, hair as free:
Such sweet neglect more taketh me
Than all th'adulteries of art.
They strike mine eyes, but not my heart.

BEN JONSON

99 UPON JULIA'S CLOTHES

When as in silks my Julia goes,
Then, then (me thinks) how sweetly flows
The liquefaction of her clothes.

Next, when I cast mine eyes and see
That brave vibration each way free,
O how that glittering taketh me!

ROBERT HERRICK

100 A CONJURATION, TO ELECTRA

By those soft tods of wool
With which the air is full:
By all those tinctures there,
That paint the hemisphere:
By dews and drizzling rain,
That swell the golden grain:
By all those sweets that be
I' the flow'ry nunnery:
By silent nights, and the
Three forms of Hecate:
By all aspects that bless
The sober sorceress,
While juice she strains, and pith
To make her philtres with:
By Time, that hastens on
Things to perfection:
And by your self, the best
Conjurement of the rest:
O my Electra! be
In love with none, but me.

ROBERT HERRICK

Thou more than most sweet glove,
Unto my more sweet love,
Suffer me to store with kisses
This empty lodging, that now misses
The pure rosy hand, that ware thee,
Whiter than the kid that bare thee.
Thou art soft, but that was softer;
Cupid's self hath kiss'd it ofter
Than e'er he did his mother's doves,
Supposing her the queen of loves,
That was thy mistress, best of gloves.

BEN JONSON

102 TO DAISIES, NOT TO SHUT SO SOON

Shut not so soon; the dull-ey'd night
   Has not as yet begun
To make a seizure on the light,
   Or to seal up the sun.

No marigolds yet closed are;
   No shadows great appear;
Nor doth the early Shepherds' Star
   Shine like a spangle here.

Stay but till my Julia close
   Her life-begetting eye;
And let the whole world then dispose
   Itself to live or die.

ROBERT HERRICK

103 CEAN DUBH DEELISH

Put your head, darling, darling, darling,
  Your darling black head my heart above;
Oh, mouth of honey, with the thyme for fragrance,
  Who, with heart in breast, could deny you love?
Oh, many and many a young girl for me is pining,
  Letting her locks of gold to the cold wind free,
For me, the foremost of our gay young fellows;
  But I'd leave a hundred, pure love, for thee!
Then put your head, darling, darling, darling,
  Your darling black head my heart above;
Oh, mouth of honey, with the thyme for fragrance,
  Who, with heart in breast, could deny you love?

SIR SAMUEL FERGUSON

104

Love, the delight of all well-thinking minds;
Delight, the fruit of virtue dearly lov'd;
Virtue, the highest good, that reason finds;
Reason, the fire wherein men's thoughts be prov'd;
  Are from the world by Nature's power bereft,
  And in one creature, for her glory, left.

Beauty, her cover is, the eyes' true pleasure;
In honour's fame she lives, the ears' sweet music;
Excess of wonder grows from her true measure;
Her worth is passion's wound, and passion's physic;
  From her true heart, clear springs of wisdom flow,
  Which imag'd in her words and deeds, men know.

Time fain would stay, that she might never leave her,
Place doth rejoice, that she must needs contain her,
Death craves of Heaven, that she may not bereave her,
The Heavens know their own, and do maintain her;
    Delight, love, reason, virtue let it be,
    To set all women light, but only she.

FULKE GREVILLE, LORD BROOKE

105 BALADE

Hide, Absalon, thy gilte tresses clear;
Ester, lay thou thy meekness all a-down;
Hide, Jonathas, all thy friendly maner;
Penalopee and Marcia Catoun,
Make of your wifehood no comparisoun;
Hide ye your beauties, Isoude and Eleyne:
My lady cometh that all this may distain.

Thy faire body, lat it not appear,
Lavine; and thou, Lucresse of Rome town;
And Polixene, that boughten love so dear,
And Cleopatre, with all thy passioun,
Hide ye your trouth of love and your renown;
And thou, Tisbe, that hast of love such pain:
My lady cometh that all this may distain.

Hero, Dido, Laudomia, all y-fere,
And Phyllis, hanging for thy Demophoun,
And Canace, espied by thy chere,
Ysiphile, betraysed with Jasoun,
Maketh of your trouthe neither boost ne soun;
Nor Ypermistre or Adriane, ye twain:
My lady cometh that all this may distain.

GEOFFREY CHAUCER

106 ON HIS MISTRESS, THE QUEEN OF BOHEMIA

You meaner beauties of the night,
  That poorly satisfy our eyes
More by your number than your light,
  You common people of the skies;
  What are you when the moon shall rise?

You curious chanters of the wood,
  That warble forth Dame Nature's lays,
Thinking your passions understood
  By your weak accents; what's your praise,
  When Philomel her voice shall raise?

You violets that first appear,
  By your pure purple mantles known
Like the proud virgins of the year,
  As if the spring were all your own;
  What are you when the rose is blown?

So, when my mistress shall be seen
  In form and beauty of her mind,
By virtue first, then choice, a Queen,
  Tell me if she were not designed
  Th' eclipse and glory of her kind?

SIR HENRY WOTTON

107

My sweetest Lesbia, let us live and love;
And, though the sager sort our deeds reprove,
Let us not weigh them: Heaven's great lamps do dive
Into their west, and straight again revive,

But, soon as once set is our little light,
Then must we sleep one ever-during night.

If all would lead their lives in love like me,
Then bloody swords and armour should not be;
No drum nor trumpet peaceful sleeps should move,
Unless alarm came from the camp of love.
But fools do live, and waste their little light,
And seek with pain their ever-during night.

When timely death my life and fortune ends,
Let not my hearse be vex'd with mourning friends,
But let all lovers, rich in triumph, come,
And with sweet pastimes grace my happy tomb;
And, Lesbia, close up thou my little light,
And crown with love my ever-during night.

THOMAS CAMPION

108 CLAIR DE LUNE

Votre âme est un paysage choisi
Que vont charmant masques et bergamasques,
Jouant du luth, et dansant, et quasi
Tristes sous leurs déguisements fantasques.

Tout en chantant sur le mode mineur
L'amour vainqueur et la vie opportune,
Ils n'ont pas l'air de croire à leur bonheur
Et leur chanson se mêle au clair de lune.

Au calme clair de lune triste et beau,
Qui fait rêver les oiseaux dans les arbres
Et sangloter d'extase les jets d'eau,
Les grands jets d'eau sveltes parmi les marbres.

PAUL VERLAINE

109 MAY TREES IN A STORM

How this year of years do I best see
These famous blossoms of the dangerous May?

In headlights wild and scattering,
Threshing in a wind of May?
    The four roads join,
HALT glitters, but I choose
      Your way.

GEOFFREY GRIGSON

110

Cupid and my Campaspe played
At cards for kisses, Cupid paid;
He stakes his quiver, bow, and arrows,
His mother's doves, and team of sparrows;
Loses them too; then, down he throws
The coral of his lip, the rose
Growing on's cheek (but none knows how);
With these, the crystal of his brow,
And then the dimple of his chin:
All these did my Campaspe win.
At last, he set her both his eyes;
She won, and Cupid blind did rise.
    O Love! has she done this to thee?
    What shall (alas!) become of me?

JOHN LYLY

III [*from* THE MERCHANT OF VENICE]

LORENZO The moon shines bright. In such a night as this,
When the sweet wind did gently kiss the trees,
And they did make no noise, in such a night
Troilus methinks mounted the Troyan walls,
And sigh'd his soul toward the Grecian tents
Where Cressid lay that night.

JESSICA   In such a night
Did Thisbe fearfully o'ertrip the dew,
And saw the lion's shadow ere himself,
And ran dismay'd away.

LORENZO   In such a night
Stood Dido with a willow in her hand
Upon the wild sea-banks, and waft her love
To come again to Carthage.

JESSICA   In such a night
Medea gather'd the enchanted herbs
That did renew old Æson.

LORENZO   In such a night
Did Jessica steal from the wealthy Jew,
And with an unthrift love did run from Venice,
As far as Belmont.

JESSICA   In such a night
Did young Lorenzo swear he lov'd her well,
Stealing her soul with many vows of faith,
And n'er a true one.

LORENZO   In such a night
Did pretty Jessica (like a little shrew)
Slander her love, and he forgave it her.

JESSICA I would out-night you did no body come:
But hark, I hear the footing of a man.

WILLIAM SHAKESPEARE

112 A BETROTHAL

Put your hand on my heart, say that you love me as
The woods upon the hills cleave to the hills' contours.

I will uphold you, trunk and shoot and flowering sheaf,
And I will hold you, roots and fruit and fallen leaf.

E. J. SCOVELL

113 LOUISA

AFTER ACCOMPANYING HER ON A MOUNTAIN EXCURSION

I met Louisa in the shade,
And, having seen that lovely Maid,
Why should I fear to say
That, nymph-like, she is fleet and strong.
And down the rocks can leap along
Like rivulets in May?

And she hath smiles to earth unknown;
Smiles, that with motion of their own
Do spread, and sink, and rise;
That come and go with endless play,
And ever, as they pass away,
Are hidden in her eyes.

She loves her fire, her cottage-home;
Yet o'er the moorland will she roam
In weather rough and bleak;
And, when against the wind she strains,
Oh! might I kiss the mountain rains
That sparkle on her cheek.

Take all that's mine 'beneath the moon,'
If I with her but half a noon
May sit beneath the walls
Of some old cave, or mossy nook,
When up she winds along the brook
To hunt the waterfalls.

WILLIAM WORDSWORTH

114

Among all lovely things my Love had been;
Had noted well the stars, all flowers that grew
About her home; but she had never seen
A glow-worm, never one, and this I knew.

While riding near her home one stormy night
A single glow-worm did I chance to espy;
I gave a fervent welcome to the sight,
And from my horse I leapt; great joy had I.

Upon a leaf the glow-worm did I lay,
To bear it with me through the stormy night:
And, as before, it shone without dismay;
Albeit putting forth a fainter light.

When to the dwelling of my Love I came,
I went into the orchard quietly;
And left the glow-worm, blessing it by name,
Laid safely by itself, beneath a tree.

The whole next day, I hoped, and hoped with fear;
At night the glow-worm shone beneath the tree;
I led my Lucy to the spot, 'Look here,'
Oh! joy it was for her, and joy for me!

WILLIAM WORDSWORTH

Wherefore peep'st thou, envious day?
  We can kiss without thee.
Lovers hate the golden ray,
  Which thou bear'st about thee.
Go and give them light that sorrow
  Or the sailor flying:
Our embraces need no morrow
  Nor our blisses eyeing.

We shall curse thy curious eye
  For thy soon betraying,
And condemn thee for a spy
  If thou catch us playing,
Get thee gone and lend thy flashes
  Where there's need of lending,
Our affections are not ashes
  Nor our pleasures ending.

Were we cold or withered here
  We would stay thee by us,
Or but one another's fear
  Then thou shouldst not fly us.
We are young, thou spoil'st our pleasure;
  Go to sea and slumber,
Darkness only gives us leisure
  Our stol'n joys to number.

ANON.

116 SHE TELLS HER LOVE WHILE HALF ASLEEP

She tells her love while half asleep,
   In the dark hours,
      With half-words whispered low:
As Earth stirs in her winter sleep
   And puts out grass and flowers
      Despite the snow,
      Despite the falling snow.

ROBERT GRAVES

117 THE RAGGED WOOD

O hurry where by water among the trees
The delicate-stepping stag and his lady sigh,
When they have but looked upon their images—
Would none had ever loved but you and I!

Or have you heard that sliding silver-shoed
Pale silver-proud queen-woman of the sky,
When the sun looked out of his golden hood?—
O that none ever loved but you and I!

O hurry to the ragged wood, for there
I will drive all those lovers out and cry—
O my share of the world, O yellow hair!
No one has ever loved but you and I.

W. B. YEATS

118

Thus saith my Chloris bright
When we of love sit down and talk together:
Beware of Love, Love is a walking sprite,
    And Love is this and that,
    And O I wot not what,
And comes and goes again, I wot not whither.
No, no, these are but bugs to breed amazing,
For in her eyes I saw his torchlight blazing.

ANON. (from the Italian of
GIOVAN BATTISTA GUARINI)

119   THEE, THEE, ONLY THEE

The dawning of morn, the daylight's sinking,
The night's long hours still find me thinking
    Of thee, thee, only thee.
When friends are met, and goblets crown'd,
    And smiles are near that once enchanted,
Unreach'd by all that sunshine round,
    My soul, like some dark spot, is haunted
    By thee, thee, only thee.

Whatever in fame's high path could waken
My spirit once is now forsaken
    For thee, thee, only thee.
Like shores by which some headlong bark
    To the ocean hurries, resting never,
Life's scenes go by me, bright or dark
    I know not, heed not, hastening ever
    To thee, thee, only thee.

I have not a joy but of thy bringing,
And pain itself seems sweet when springing
    From thee, thee, only thee.
Like spells that nought on earth can break,
    Till lips that know the charm have spoken,
This heart, howe'er the world may wake
    Its grief, its scorn, can but be broken
        By thee, thee, only thee.

THOMAS MOORE

120 AUTUMN IDLENESS

This sunlight shames November where he grieves
    In dead red leaves, and will not let him shun
    The day, though bough with bough be over-run.
But with a blessing every glade receives
High salutation; while from hillock-eaves
    The deer gaze calling, dappled white and dun,
    As if, being foresters of old, the sun
Had marked them with the shade of forest-leaves.

Here dawn to-day unveiled her magic glass;
    Here noon now gives the thirst and takes the dew;
Till eve bring rest when other good things pass.
    And here the lost hours the lost hours renew
While I still lead my shadow o'er the grass,
    Nor know, for longing, that which I should do.

D. G. ROSSETTI

121 THE SPIRIT'S EPOCHS

Not in the crises of events,
   Of compass'd hopes, or fears fulfill'd,
Or acts of gravest consequence,
   Are life's delight and depth reveal'd.
The day of days was not the day;
   That went before, or was postponed;
The night Death took our lamp away
   Was not the night on which we groan'd.
I drew my bride, beneath the moon,
   Across my threshold; happy hour!
But, ah, the walk that afternoon
   We saw the water-flags in flower!

COVENTRY PATMORE

122 SUR LES MARCHES DU PALAIS

(FOLKSONG)

Sur les march' du palais
Sur les march' du palais
Y a un' tant belle fille
      Lon la
Y a un' tant belle fille

Elle a tant d'amoureux
Elle a tant d'amoureux
Qu'elle ne sait lequel prendre
      Lon la
Qu'elle ne sait lequel prendre

C'est un p'tit cordonnier
C'est un p'tit cordonnier
Qu'a eu sa préférence
     Lon la
Qu'a eu sa préférence

C'est en lui chaussant l'pied
C'est en lui chaussant l'pied
Qu'il lui fit sa demande
     Lon la
Qu'il lui fit sa demande

La bell' si tu voulais
La bell' si tu voulais
Nous dormirions ensemble
     Lon la
Nous dormirions ensemble

Dans un grand lit carré
Dans un grand lit carré
Aux belles taies blanches
     Lon la
Aux belles taies blanches

Aux quatre coins du lit
Aux quatre coins du lit
Quat' bouquets de pervenches
     Lon la
Quat' bouquets de pervenches

Dans le mitan du lit
Dans le mitan du lit
La rivière est profonde
     Lon la
La rivière est profonde

Tous les chevaux du Roi
Tous les chevaux du Roi
Pourraient y boire ensemble
　　Lon la
Pourraient y boire ensemble

Nous y pourrions dormir
Nous y pourrions dormir
Jusqu'à la fin du monde
　　Lon la
Jusqu'à la fin du monde.

123   THE OUTLAW OF LOCH LENE

O many a day have I made good ale in the glen,
That came not of stream, or malt, like the brewing of men.
My bed was the ground, my roof, the greenwood above,
And the wealth that I sought—one far kind glance from my love.

Alas! on that night when the horses I drove from the field,
That I was not near from terror my angel to shield.
She stretched forth her arms,—her mantle she flung to the wind,
And swam o'er Loch Lene, her outlawed lover to find.

O would that a freezing sleet-winged tempest did sweep,
And I and my love were alone far off on the deep!
I'd ask not a ship, or a bark, or pinnace to save,—
With her hand round my waist, I'd fear not the wind or the wave.

'Tis down by the lake where the wild tree fringes its sides,
The maid of my heart, the fair one of Heaven resides—
I think as at eve she wanders its mazes along,
The birds go to sleep by the sweet wild twist of her song.

JEREMIAH JOSEPH CALLANAN

124

On the smooth brow and clustering hair
   Myrtle and rose! your wreath combine;
The duller olive I would wear,
   Its constancy, its peace, be mine.

WALTER SAVAGE LANDOR

125 CALLED PROUD

If I am proud, you surely know,
Ianthe! who has made me so,
And only should condemn the pride
That can arise from aught beside.

WALTER SAVAGE LANDOR

126

O Divine Star of Heaven,
Thou in power above the seven:
Thou sweet kindler of desires,
Till they grow to mutual fires:
Thou, O gentle Queen, that art
Curer of each wounded heart:
Thou the fuel, and the flame;
Thou in Heaven, and here the same:
Thou the wooer, and the woo'd:
Thou the hunger, and the food:

Thou the prayer, and the pray'd;
Thou what is, or shall be said:
Thou still young, and golden tressed,
Make me by thy answer blessed.

JOHN FLETCHER

127 PERSPECTIVE

What seems to us for us is true.
　　The planet has no proper light,
And yet, when Venus is in view,
　　No primal star is half so bright.

COVENTRY PATMORE

128 [BALADE SIMPLE]

Fairest of stars, that with your persant light
And with the cherishing of your streames clear,
Causen in love heartes to be light
Only thorough shining of your glad sphere,
Now laud and price, O Venus, lady dear,
Be to your name, that have withoute sin
This man fortuned his lady for to win.

Willy planet, O Esperus, so bright,
That woeful heartes can appease and steer,
And ever are ready thorough your grace and might
To help all those that buy love so dear,
And have power heartes to set on fire,
Honour to you of all that ben herein,
That have this man his lady made to win.

O mighty goddess, day star after night,
Gladding the morrow when ye do appear,
To void darkness thorough freshness of your sight,
Only with twinkling of your pleasant cheer,
To you we thank, lovers that been here,
That this man—and never for to twin—
Fortuned have his lady for to win.

JOHN LYDGATE

129

Whirl'd off at last, for speech I sought,
    To keep shy Love in countenance;
But, whilst I vainly tax'd my thought,
    Her voice deliver'd mine from trance:
'Look, is not this a pretty shawl,
    'Aunt's parting gift.' 'She's always kind,'
'The new wing spoils Sir John's old Hall:
    'You'll see it, if you pull the blind.'

I drew the silk: in heaven the night
    Was dawning; lovely Venus shone,
In languishment of tearful light,
    Swathed by the red breath of the sun.

COVENTRY PATMORE

130 L'HEURE DU BERGER

La lune est rouge au brumeux horizon;
Dans un brouillard qui danse, la prairie
S'endort fumeuse, et la grenouille crie
Par les joncs verts où circule un frisson;

Les fleurs des eaux referment leurs corolles;
Des peupliers profilent aux lointains,
Droits et serrés, leurs spectres incertains;
Vers les buissons errent les lucioles;

Les chats-huants s'éveillent, et sans bruit
Rament l'air noir avec leurs ailes lourdes,
Et le zénith s'emplit de lueurs sourdes.
Blanche, Vénus émerge, et c'est la Nuit.

PAUL VERLAINE

131 LOVE'S IMMATURITY

Not weaned yet, without comprehension loving,
We feed at breasts of love; like a still cat
That wears and loves the fire in peace, till moving
She slips off fire and love, to cross the mat

As new as birth; so by default denying
House-roof and human friends that come and go,
The landscape of life's dream. Antelopes flying
Over his wild earth serve the lion so.

We are blind children who answer with love
A warmth and sweetness. Those even we love most
We sleep within their lives like cats, and rove
Out in the night, and late return and coast

Their souls like furniture. Oh, life should give
Light till we understand they live, they live.

E. J. SCOVELL

132 IN A WOOD

I saw my love, younger than primroses,
Sleeping in a wood.
Why do I love best what sleep uncloses,
Sorrowful creaturehood?

Dark, labyrinthine with anxiety,
His face is like coiled infancy;
Like parched and wrinkled buds, the first of the year,
Thrown out on winter air.

Stiller than close eyes of a nested bird,
Clear from the covert of his sleeping,
One looked out that knows no human word
But gives me love and weeping.

E. J. SCOVELL

3

THE PLAGUES OF LOVING

133

Orpheus I am, come from the deeps below,
To thee, fond man, the plagues of love to show:
To the fair fields where loves eternal dwell
There's none that come, but first they pass through hell:
    Hark and beware, unless thou hast lov'd ever,
    Belov'd again, thou shalt see those joys never.

Hark how they groan that died despairing,
    O take heed then:
Hark how they howl for over-daring,
    All these were men.

They that be fools, and die for fame
    They lose their name;
And they that bleed
    Hark how they speed.

Now in cold frosts, now scorching fires
They sit, and curse their lost desires:
Nor shall these souls be free from pain and fears,
Till women waft them over in their tears.

JOHN FLETCHER

134

    Whither shall I go
        To escape from folly?
    For now there's love I know,
        Or else 'tis melancholly,
            Heigh, heigho.

Yonder lies the snow,
    But my heart cannot melt it;
Love shoots from his bow,
    And my poor heart hath felt it,
            Heigh, heigho.

ANON.

135

April is in my mistress' face,
And July in her eyes hath place,
Within her bosom is September,
But in her heart a cold December.

ANON. (from the Italian)

136

O Friendship! Friendship! the shell of Aphrodite
Lies always at the bottom of thy warm and limpid waters.

WALTER SAVAGE LANDOR

137

Wand'ring in this place as in a wilderness,
No comfort have I nor yet assurance,
Desolate of joy, repleat with sadness:
Wherefore I may say, *O deus, deus,*
Non est dolor, sicut dolor meus.

ANON.

Shall I come, sweet Love, to thee,
  When the ev'ning beams are set?
Shall I not excluded be?
   Will you find no fained let?
    Let me not, for pity, more,
    Tell the long hours at your door.

Who can tell what thief or foe,
  In the covert of the night,
For his prey, will work my woe,
  Or through wicked foul despite:
    So may I die unredress'd,
    Ere my long love be possess'd.

But, to let such dangers pass,
  Which a lover's thoughts disdain,
'Tis enough in such a place
  To attend love's joys in vain.
    Do not mock me in thy bed,
    While these cold nights freeze me dead.

THOMAS CAMPION

139 SONNET

Fra banc to banc, fra wod to wod, I rin
Ourhailit with my feble fantasie,
Lyc til a leif that fallis from a trie
Or til a reid ourblawin with the wind.
Twa gods gyds me: the ane of tham is blind,
Ye, and a bairn brocht up in vanitie;
The nixt a wyf ingenrit of the se,
And lichter nor a dauphin with hir fin.

Unhappie is the man for evirmaire
That teils the sand and sawis in the aire;
Bot twyse unhappier is he, I lairn,
That feidis in his hairt a mad desyre,
And follows on a woman throw the fyre,
Led be a blind and teichit be a bairn.

MARK ALEXANDER BOYD

140 THE RESOLUTE COURTIER

Prithee, say aye or no;
If thou'lt not have me, tell me so;
I cannot stay,
Nor will I wait upon
A smile or frown.
If thou wilt have me, say;
Then I am thine, or else I am mine own.

Be white or black; I hate
Dependence on a checkered fate;
Let go, or hold;
Come, either kiss or not:
Now to be hot,
And then again as cold,
Is a fantastic fever you have got.

A tedious woo is base,
And worse by far than a long grace:
For whilst we stay,
Our lingering spoils the roast,
Or stomach's lost;
Nor can, nor will I stay;
For if I sup not quickly, I will fast.

Whilst we are fresh and stout
And vigorous, let us to 't:
    Alas, what good
From wrinkled man appears,
    Gelded with years,
When his thin wheyish blood
Is far less comfortable than his tears?

THOMAS SHIPMAN

141

I laid me down upon a bank
Where love lay sleeping.
I heard among the rushes dank
Weeping, weeping.

Then I went to the heath and the wild,
To the thistles and thorns of the waste,
And they told me how they were beguil'd,
Driven out, and compell'd to be chaste.

WILLIAM BLAKE

142 THE GARDEN OF LOVE

I went to the Garden of Love,
And saw what I never had seen:
A Chapel was built in the midst,
Where I used to play on the green.

And the gates of this Chapel were shut,
And 'Thou shalt not' writ over the door;
So I turn'd to the Garden of Love
That so many sweet flowers bore;

And I saw it was filled with graves,
And tomb-stones where flowers should be;
And Priests in black gowns were walking their rounds,
And binding with briars my joys and desires.

WILLIAM BLAKE

143

As it fell upon a day,
In the merry month of May,
Sitting in a pleasant shade,
Which a grove of myrtles made,
Beasts did leap, and birds did sing,
Trees did grow, and plants did spring:
Every thing did banish moan,
Save the Nightingale alone.
She, poor bird, as all forlorn,
Lean'd her breast against a thorn,
And there sung the dolefull'st ditty,
That to hear it was great pity.
Fie, fie, fie, now would she cry;
Teru, teru, by and by:
That to hear her so complain,
Scarce I could from tears refrain:
For her griefs so lively shown
Made me think upon mine own.
Ah (thought I) thou mourn'st in vain,
None takes pity on thy pain:

Senseless trees, they cannot hear thee,
Ruthless beasts, they will not cheer thee;
King Pandion, he is dead,
All thy friends are lapp'd in lead.
All thy fellow birds do sing,
Careless of thy sorrowing:
Even so, poor bird, like thee,
None alive will pity me.

RICHARD BARNFIELD

144 LOVE WITHOUT HOPE

Love without hope, as when the young bird-catcher
Swept off his tall hat to the Squire's own daughter,
So let the imprisoned larks escape and fly
Singing about her head, as she rode by.

▸ ROBERT GRAVES

145 TO A LADY

Sweit rois of vertew and of gentilnes,
Delytsum lyllie of everie lustynes,
    Richest in bontie and in bewtie cleir,
    And everie vertew that is held most deir,
Except onlie that ye are mercyles.

In to your garthe this day I did persew,
Their saw I flowris that fresche wer of hew;
    Baith quhyte and reid moist lusty wer to seyne,
    And halsum herbis upone stalkis grene;
Yit leif nor flour fynd could I nane of rew.

I dout that Merche, with his caild blastis keyne,
Hes slane this gentill herbe that I of mene,
    Quhois petewous deithe dois to my hart sic pane
    That I wald mak to plant his rute agane,
So confortand his levis unto me bene.

WILLIAM DUNBAR

146

Fair is my love that feeds among the lilies,
    The lilies growing in the pleasant garden,
Where Cupid's mount, that well-beloved hill is,
    And where that little god himself is warden.
See where my love sits in the beds of spices,
    Beset all round with camphor, myrrh and roses,
And interlac'd with curious devices,
    Which her from all the world apart incloses.
There doth she tune her lute for her delight,
    And with sweet music makes the ground to move,
Whilst I (poor I) do sit in heavy plight,
    Wailing alone my unrespected love,
Not daring to rush into so rare a place,
That gives to her, and she to it, a grace.

BARTHOLOMEW GRIFFIN

147

Merciless Love, whom nature hath denied
The use of eyes, lest thou shouldst take a pride
And glory in thy murthers:
Why am I

That never yet transgress'd thy deity,
Never broke vow, from whose eyes never
Flew disdainful dart,
Whose hard heart none e'er slew,
Thus ill rewarded?

Thou art young and fair,
Thy Mother soft and gentle as the air,
Thy holy fire still burning, blown with prayer.
Then, everlasting Love, restrain thy will,
'Tis god-like to have power, but not to kill.

JOHN FLETCHER

148 THE TRIPLE FOOL

I am two fools, I know,
For loving, and for saying so
    In whining poetry;
But where's that wise man, that would not be I,
    If she would not deny?
Then as th'earth's inward narrow crooked lanes
Do purge sea water's fretful salt away,
    I thought, if I could draw my pains
Through rhyme's vexations, I should them allay,
Grief brought to numbers cannot be so fierce,
For, he tames it, that fetters it in verse.

    But when I have done so,
Some man, his art and voice to show,
    Doth set and sing my pain,
And, by delighting many, frees again
    Grief, which verse did restrain.

To Love, and Grief, tribute of verse belongs,
But not of such as pleases when 'tis read,
  Both are increased by such songs:
For both their triumphs so are published,
And I, which was two fools, do so grow three;
Who are a little wise, the best fools be.

JOHN DONNE

149

As fair as morn, as fresh as May,
A pretty grace in saying Nay,
Smil'st thou, sweet heart? Then sing and say
          Ta na na no.
But O that love-enchanting eye!
Lo here my doubtful doom I try:
Tell me, my sweet, live I or die?
She smiles. Ah, she frowns. Ay me, I die.

ANON.

150

If this be love, to draw a weary breath,
To paint on floods till the shore cry to th'air;
With downward looks, still reading on the earth
The sad memorials of my love's despair:
  If this be love, to war against my soul,
Lie down to wail, rise up to sigh and grieve,
The never-resting stone of care to roll,
Still to complain my griefs whilst none relieve:

If this be love, to clothe me with dark thoughts,
Haunting untrodden paths to wail apart;
My pleasures horror, music tragic notes,
Tears in mine eyes and sorrow at my heart.
If this be love, to live a living death,
Then do I love and draw this weary breath.

SAMUEL DANIEL

151 SONG: I WOULD NOT FEIGN
A SINGLE SIGH

I would not feign a single sigh
Nor weep a single tear for thee,
The soul within these orbs burns dry,
A desert spreads where love should be.
I would not be a worm to crawl
A wreathing suppliant in thy way;
For love is life, is heaven, and all
The beams of an immortal day.

For sighs are idle things, and vain,
And tears for idiots vainly fall,
I would not kiss thy face again
Nor round thy shining slippers crawl.
Love is the honey, not the bee,
Nor would I turn its sweets to gall
For all the beauty found in thee,
Thy lily neck, rose cheek, and all.

I would not feign a single tale
Thy kindness or thy love to seek,
Nor sigh for Jenny of the Vale,
Her ruby smile or rosy cheek.

I would not have a pain to own
   For those dark curls, and those bright eyes.
A frowning lip, a heart of stone,
   False love and folly I despise.

JOHN CLARE

152

Loving in truth, and fain in verse my love to show,
That she, dear she, might take some pleasure of my pain:
Pleasure might cause her read, reading might make her know,
Knowledge might pity win, and pity grace obtain,
   I sought fit words to paint the blackest face of woe,
Studying inventions fine, her wits to entertain:
Oft turning others' leaves to see if thence would flow
Some fresh and fruitful showers upon my sun-burn'd brain.
   But words came halting forth, wanting Invention's stay,
Invention, Nature's child, fled step-dame Study's blows,
And others' feet still seem'd but strangers in my way.
Thus great with child to speak, and helpless in my throes,
   Biting my trewand pen, beating myself for spite,
   Fool, said my Muse to me, look in thy heart and write.

SIR PHILIP SIDNEY

153

Shall I abide this jesting?
I weep, and she's a-feasting.
O cruel fancy that so doth blind thee
To love one doth not mind thee.

Can I abide this prancing?
I weep, and she's a-dancing.
O cruel fancy so to betray me,
Thou goest about to slay me.

ANON.

154 LADY GREENSLEEVES

Alas, my love, ye do me wrong,
To cast me off disc'urteously:
And I have loved you so long,
Delighting in your company.

Greensleeves was all my joy,
Greensleeves was my delight:
Greensleeves was my heart of gold,
And who but Lady Greensleeves.

I have been ready at your hand,
To grant what ever you would crave.
I have both waged life and land,
Your love and good will for to have.

Greensleeves was all my joy, etc.

I bought thee kerchers to thy head,
That were wrought fine and gallantly:
I kept thee both at board and bed,
Which cost my purse well favouredly,

I bought thee petticoats of the best,
The cloth so fine as fine might be:
I gave thee jewels for thy chest,
And all this cost I spent on thee.

Thy smock of silk, both fair and white,
  With gold embroidered gorgeously:
Thy petticoat of sendal right:
  And thus I bought thee gladly.

Thy girdle of gold so red,
  With pearls bedecked sumptuously:
The like no other lasses had,
  And yet thou wouldst not love me,

Thy purse and eke thy gay guilt knives,
  Thy pincase gallant to the eye:
No better wore the burgess wives,
  And yet thou wouldst not love me.

Thy crimson stockings all of silk,
  With gold all wrought above the knee,
Thy pumps as white as was the milk,
  And yet thou wouldst not love me.

Thy gown was of the grossy green,
  Thy sleeves of satin hanging by:
Which made thee be our harvest Queen,
  And yet thou wouldst not love me.

Thy garters fringed with the gold,
  And silver aglets hanging by,
Which made thee blithe for to behold,
  And yet thou wouldst not love me.

My gayest gelding I thee gave,
  To ride where ever liked thee,
No Lady ever was so brave,
  And yet thou wouldst not love me.

My men were clothed all in green,
  And they did ever wait on thee:
All this was gallant to be seen,
  And yet thou wouldst not love me.

They set thee up, they took thee down,
  They served thee with humility,
Thy foot might not once touch the ground,
  And yet thou wouldst not love me.

For every morning when thou rose,
  I sent thee dainties orderly:
To cheer thy stomach from all woes,
  And yet thou wouldst not love me.

Thou couldst desire no earthly thing.
  But still thou hadst it readily:
Thy music still to play and sing,
  And yet thou wouldst not love me.

And who did pay for all this gear,
  That thou didst spend when pleased thee?
Even I that am rejected here,
  And thou disdainst to love me.

Well, I will pray to God on high,
  That thou my constancy mayst see:
And that yet once before I die,
  Thou wilt vouchsafe to love me.

Greensleeves now farewell, adieu,
  God I pray to prosper thee:
For I am still thy lover true,
  Come once again and love me.

ANON.

155

Brown is my Love, but graceful;
And each renowned whiteness
Matched with thy lovely brown loseth its brightness.

Fair is my Love, but scornful:
Yet I have seen despised
Dainty white lilies, and sad flowers well prized.

ANON. (from the Italian)

156

Genévres herissez, et vous, houx espineux,
L'un hoste des deserts, et l'autre d'un bocage,
Lierre, le tapis d'un bel antre sauvage,
Sources qui bouillonnez d'un surgeon sablonneux;
Pigeons, qui vous baisez d'un baiser savoureux,
Tourtres qui lamentez d'un eternel vefvage,
Rossignols ramagers, qui d'un plaisant langage
Nuict et jour rechantez vos versets amoureux;
Vous à la gorge rouge, estrangere Arondelle,
Si vous voyez aller ma Nymphe en ce Printemps
Pour cueillir des bouquets par ceste herbe nouvelle,
Dites luy, pour-neant que sa grace j'attens,
Et que pour ne souffrir le mal que j'ay pour elle,
J'ay mieux aimé mourir que languir si long temps.

PIERRE DE RONSARD

She that holds me under the laws of love
  On whom my mournful verse so oft complains
For those strange griefs that I through wrong do prove,
  She is the court wherein my life remains,
She is my prince of whom I would deserve
  And she alone to me can favour lend.
She hath for courtiers thousands that do serve
  And only on her eyes for looks attend,
Unto her love we would as fain aspire
  As others would in court to honours rise,
And as disgrace makes courtiers to retire
  So do her frowns cause malcontents likewise.
Like to the court she is unconstant and unkind,
  But from the court differs in this alone,
That in the court men hope reward to find,
  But following her such hope remaineth none.

SIR ARTHUR GORGES

I, with whose colours Myra dress'd her head,
I, that ware posies of her own hand-making,
I, that mine own name in the chimneys read
By Myra finely wrought ere I was waking:
    Must I look on, in hope time coming may
    With change bring back my turn again to play?

I, that on Sunday at the church-stile found
A garland sweet, with true-love knots in flowers,
Which I to wear about mine arm was bound,
That each of us might know that all was ours:

Must I now lead an idle life in wishes?
And follow Cupid for his loaves, and fishes?

I, that did wear the ring her mother left,
I, for whose love she gloried to be blamed,
I, with whose eyes her eyes committed theft,
I, who did make her blush when I was named;
    Must I lose ring, flowers, blush, theft and go naked,
    Watching with sighs, till dead love be awaked?

I, that when drowsy Argus fell asleep,
Like jealousy o'erwatched with desire,
Was ever warned modesty to keep,
While her breath, speaking, kindled Nature's fire:
    Must I look on a-cold, while others warm them?
    Do Vulcan's brothers in such fine nets arm them?

Was it for this that I might Myra see
Washing the water, with her beauties, white?
Yet would she never write her love to me;
Thinks wit of change, while thoughts are in delight?
    Mad girls must safely love, as they may leave,
    No man can print a kiss, lines may deceive.

FULKE GREVILLE, LORD BROOKE

159

He that hath no mistress, must not wear a favour,
He that woos a mistress, must serve before he have her,
He that hath no bedfellow, must lie alone,
And he that hath no lady, must be content with Joan,
And so must I, for why alas my love and I am parted,
False Cupid, I will have thee whipt, and have thy mother carted.

ANON.

160

Sweet trees who shade this mould
Of earth, your heads down bend,
　When you those eyes behold
Of my best-loved friend.
　Fair stars, whose bright appear
Doth beautify the sky,
　Why wake you not my dear,
If he asleeping lie?

　You birds, whose warblings prove
Aurora draweth near,
　Go fly, and tell my love,
That I expect him here.
　The night doth posting move,
Yet comes he not again;
　God grant some other love
Do not my love detain.

JAMES MABBE (from the Spanish)

161

Nothing but no and I, and I and no,
How falls it out so strangely you reply?
I tell ye, fair, I'll not be answered so,
With this affirming no, denying I.
I say, I love, you sleightly answer, I:
I say, you love, you pule me out a no:
I say, I die, you echo me with I:
Save me, I cry, you sigh me out a no;

Must woe and I have nought but no and I?
No I am I, if I no more can have;
Answer no more, with silence make reply,
And let me take myself what I do crave,
   Let no and I, with I and you be so:
   Then answer no and I, and I and no.

MICHAEL DRAYTON

162

Take, O take those lips away,
   That so sweetly were forsworn,
And those eyes: the break of day
   Lights that do mislead the morn;
But my kisses bring again, bring again,
Seals of love, but seal'd in vain, seal'd in vain.

WILLIAM SHAKESPEARE

163 I'LL NEVER LOVE THEE MORE

My dear and only love, I pray
   That little world of thee
Be governed by no other sway
   Than purest monarchy;
For if confusion have a part
   (Which virtuous souls abhor),
And hold a synod in thine heart,
   I'll never love thee more.

Like Alexander I will reign,
    And I will reign alone;
My thoughts did evermore disdain
    A rival on my throne.
He either fears his fate too much,
    Or his deserts are small,
That dares not put it to the touch,
    To gain or lose it all.

And in the empire of thine heart,
    Where I should solely be,
If others do pretend a part
    Or dare to vie with me,
Or if Committees thou erect,
    And go on such a score,
I'll laugh and sing at thy neglect,
    And never love thee more.

But if thou wilt prove faithful then,
    And constant of thy word,
I'll make thee glorious by my pen
    And famous by my sword;
I'll serve thee in such noble ways
    Was never heard before;
I'll crown and deck thee all with bays,
    And love thee more and more.

JAMES GRAHAM, MARQUIS OF MONTROSE

164 A BROKEN APPOINTMENT

        You did not come,
And marching Time drew on, and wore me numb.—
Yet less for loss of your dear presence there
Than that I thus found lacking in your make

That high compassion which can overbear
Reluctance for pure lovingkindness' sake
Grieved I, when, as the hope-hour stroked its sum
       You did not come.

       You love not me,
And love alone can lend you loyalty;
—I know and knew it. But, unto the store
Of human deeds divine in all but name,
Was it not worth a little hour or more
To add yet this: Once you, a woman, came
To soothe a time-torn man; even though it be
       You love not me?

THOMAS HARDY

165

With how sad steps, O Moon, thou climb'st the skies,
  How silently, and with how wan a face,
  What, may it be that even in heav'nly place
That busy archer his sharp arrows tries?
Sure if that long with love acquainted eyes
  Can judge of love, thou feel'st a lover's case;
  I read it in thy looks, thy languish'd grace,
To me that feel the like, thy state descries.
  Then ev'n of fellowship, O Moon, tell me
Is constant love deem'd there but want of wit?
Are beauties there as proud as here they be?
Do they above love to be lov'd, and yet
  Those lovers scorn whom that love doth possess?
  Do they call virtue there ungratefulness?

SIR PHILIP SIDNEY

Dear, why make you more of a dog than me?
    If he do love, I burn, I burn in love:
    If he wait well, I never thence would move:
If he be fair, yet but a dog can be.
Little he is, so little worth is he;
    He barks, my songs thine own voice oft doth prove:
    Bidd'n, perhaps he fetcheth thee a glove,
But I unbid, fetch even my soul to thee.
    Yet while I languish, him that bosom clips,
That lap doth lap, nay lets, in spite of spite,
This sour-breath'd mate taste of those sugar'd lips.
Alas, if you grant only such delight
    To witless things, then Love I hope (since wit
    Becomes a clog) will soon ease me of it.

SIR PHILIP SIDNEY

167 LIKE THE TOUCH OF RAIN

Like the touch of rain she was
On a man's flesh and hair and eyes
When the joy of walking thus
Has taken him by surprise:

With the love of the storm he burns,
He sings, he laughs, well I know how,
But forgets when he returns
As I shall not forget her 'Go now.'

Those two words shut a door
Between me and the blessed rain
That was never shut before
And will not open again.

EDWARD THOMAS

168

What, have I thus betrayed my liberty?
  Can those black beams such burning marks engrave
  In my free side? or am I born a slave,
Whose neck becomes such yoke of tyranny?
Or want I sense to feel my misery?
  Or sprite, disdain of such disdain to have?
  Who for long faith, tho' daily help I crave,
May get no alms but scorn of beggary.
  Virtue, awake. Beauty but beauty is,
I may, I must, I can, I will, I do
Leave following that, which it is gain to miss.
Let her go. Soft, but here she comes. Go to,
  Unkind, I love you not: O me, that eye
  Doth make my heart give to my tongue the lie.

SIR PHILIP SIDNEY

169   A LOVE SONNET

I loved a lass, a fair one,
    As fair as e'er was seen;
She was indeed a rare one,
    Another Sheba queen.

But fool as then I was,
  I thought she loved me too,
But now alas she's left me,
  Falero, lero, loo.

Her hair like gold did glister,
  Each eye was like a star;
She did surpass her sister,
  Which passed all others far.
She would me honey call,
  She'd, O she'd kiss me too;
But now alas she's left me,
  Falero, lero, loo.

In summer time to Medley
  My love and I would go;
The boatmen there stood ready,
  My love and I to row.
For cream there would we call,
  For cakes, and for prunes too,
But now alas she's left me,
  Falero, lero, loo.

Many a merry meeting
  My love and I have had;
She was my only sweeting,
  She made my heart full glad,
The tears stood in her eyes,
  Like to the morning dew,
But now alas she's left me,
  Falero, lero, loo.

And as abroad we walked,
  As lovers' fashion is,
Oft as we sweetly talked
  The Sun should steal a kiss:

The wind upon her lips
  Likewise most sweetly blew;
But now alas she's left me,
  Falero, lero, loo.

Her cheeks were like the cherry,
  Her skin as white as snow,
When she was blithe and merry,
  She angel-like did show.
Her waist exceeding small,
  The fives did fit her shoe;
But now alas she's left me,
  Falero, lero, loo.

In summer time or winter
  She had her heart's desire;
I still did scorn to stint her
  From sugar, sack, or fire:
The world went round about,
  No cares we ever knew,
But now alas she's left me,
  Falero, lero, loo.

As we walked home together
  At midnight through the town,
To keep away the weather
  O'er her I'd cast my gown.
No cold my Love should feel,
  Whate'er the heavens could do;
But now alas she's left me,
  Falero, lero, loo.

Like doves we would be billing,
  And clip and kiss so fast;
Yet she would be unwilling
  That I should kiss the last;

They're Judas kisses now,
    Since that they prov'd untrue.
For now alas she's left me,
    Falero, lero, loo.

To maidens' vows and swearing
    Henceforth no credit give,
You may give them the hearing,
    But never them believe.
They are as false as fair,
    Unconstant, frail, untrue;
For mine alas has left me,
    Falero, lero, loo.

'Twas I that paid for all things,
    'Twas others drank the wine,
I cannot now recall things,
    Live but a fool to pine.
'Twas I that beat the bush,
    The bird to others flew,
For she alas hath left me,
    Falero, lero, loo.

If ever that Dame Nature,
    For this false lover's sake,
Another pleasing creature
    Like unto her would make,
Let her remember this,
    To make the other true;
For this alas hath left me,
    Falero, lero, loo.

No riches now can raise me,
    No want make me despair,
No misery amaze me,
    Nor yet for want I care:

I have lost a world itselfe,
        My earthly heaven, adieu,
    Since she alas hath left me,
        Falero, lero, loo.

GEORGE WITHER

170   THE LOVER COMPARETH HIS STATE
TO A SHIP IN PERILOUS STORM
TOSSED ON THE SEA

My galley charged with forgetfulness,
Thorough sharp seas in winter nights doth pass
Tween rock and rock, and eke mine enemy, alas,
That is my lord, steereth with cruelness,
And every oar a thought in readiness,
As though that death were light in such a case.
An endless wind doth tear the sail apace,
Of forced sighs and trusty fearfulness.
A rain of tears, a cloud of dark disdain,
Hath done the weared cords great hinderance;
Wreathed with error and eke with ignorance.
The stars be hid that led me to this pain;
Drowned is reason that should me confort,
And I remain despairing of the port.

SIR THOMAS WYATT (from the Italian of PETRACH)

Behold, love, thy power how she despiseth!
My great pain how little she regardeth!
   The holy oath, whereof she taketh no cure,
   Broken she hath; and yet she bideth sure
Right at her ease and little she dreadeth.
Weaponed thou art, and she unarmed sitteth;
To the disdainful her life she leadeth,
   To me spiteful without cause or measure,
     Behold, love.

I am in hold: if pity thee moveth,
Go bend thy bow, that stony hearts breaketh,
   And with some stroke revenge the displeasure
   Of thee and him, that sorrow doth endure,
And, as his lord, the lowly entreateth.
     Behold, love.

SIR THOMAS WYATT

172 LOVE'S DEITY

I long to talk with some old lover's ghost,
   Who died before the God of Love was born:
I cannot think that he, who then lov'd most,
   Sunk so low, as to love one which did scorn.
But since this god produc'd a destiny,
And that vice-nature, custom, lets it be,
   I must love her, that loves not me.

Sure, they which made him god, meant not so much,
   Nor he, in his young godhead practis'd it;
But when an even flame two hearts did touch,
   His office was indulgently to fit

Actives to passives. Correspondency
Only his subject was; it cannot be
   Love, till I love her, that loves me.

But every modern god will now extend
   His vast prerogative, as far as Jove.
To rage, to lust, to write to, to commend,
   All is the purlieu of the God of Love.
Oh were we waken'd by this tyranny
To ungod this child again, it could not be
   I should love her, who loves not me.

Rebel and atheist too, why murmur I,
   As though I felt the worst that love could do?
Love might make me leave loving, or might try
   A deeper plague, to make her love me too,
Which, since she loves before, I am loth to see;
Falsehood is worse than hate; and that must be,
   If she whom I love, should love me.

JOHN DONNE

173

What should I say
Since faith is dead,
And truth alway
From you is fled?
Should I be led
With doubleness?
   Nay, nay, mistress!

I promised you
And you promised me
To be as true
As I would be;

But since I see
Your double heart,
　Farewell my part!

For though to take
It is not my mind
But to forsake—
I am not blind—
And as I find
So will I trust.
　Farewell, unjust!

Can ye say nay?
But you said
That I alway
Should be obeyed;
And thus betrayed
Or that I wist—
　Farewell, unkissed!

SIR THOMAS WYATT

174

Who so list to hunt, I know where is an hind,
But as for me, helas, I may no more:
The vain travail hath wearied me so sore,
I ame of them that farthest cometh behind;
Yet may I by no means my wearied mind
Draw from the deer: but as she fleeth afore,
Fainting I follow, I leave off therefore,
Since in a net I seek to hold the wind.
Who list her hunt, I put him out of doubt,

As well as I may spend his time in vain:
And, graven with diamonds, in letters plain,
There is written, her fair neck round about:
Noli me tangere, for Caesar's I ame,
And wild for to hold, though I seem tame.

SIR THOMAS WYATT

175 THE LOVER COMPLAINETH THE UNKINDNESS OF HIS LOVE

My lute awake! perform the last
Labour that thou and I shall waste,
And end that I have now begun;
For when this song is sung and past,
My lute be still, for I have done.

As to be heard where ear is none,
As lead to grave in marble stone,
My song may pierce her heart as soon;
Should we then sigh, or sing, or moan?
No, no, my lute, for I have done.

The rocks do not so cruelly
Repulse the waves continually,
As she my suit and affection,
So that I am past remedy:
Whereby my lute and I have done.

Proud of the spoil that thou hast got
Of simple hearts thorough love's shot,
By whom, unkind, thou hast them won,
Think not he hath his bow forgot,
Although my lute and I have done.

Vengeance shall fall on thy disdain,
That makest but game on earnest pain;
Think not alone under the sun
Unquit to cause thy lovers plain,
Although my lute and I have done.

Perchance thee lie withered and old,
The winter nights that are so cold,
Plaining in vain unto the moon;
Thy wishes then dare not be told;
Care then who list, for I have done.

And then may chance thee to repent
The time that thou hast lost and spent
To cause thy lovers sigh and swoon;
Then shalt thou know beauty but lent,
And wish and want as I have done.

Now cease, my lute! this is the last
Labour that thou and I shall waste,
And ended is that we begun;
Now is this song both sung and past:
My lute, be still, for I have done.

SIR THOMAS WYATT

176 THE FOLLY OF BEING COMFORTED

One that is ever kind said yesterday:
'Your well-beloved's hair has threads of grey,
And little shadows come about her eyes;
Time can but make it easier to be wise
Though now it seems impossible, and so
All that you need is patience.'

Heart cries, 'No,

I have not a crumb of comfort, not a grain.
Time can but make her beauty over again:
Because of that great nobleness of hers
The fire that stirs about her, when she stirs,
Burns but more clearly. O she had not these ways
When all the wild summer was in her gaze.'

O heart! O heart! if she'd but turn her head,
You'd know the folly of being comforted.

W. B. YEATS

177

When thou must home to shades of underground,
And there arriv'd, a new admired guest,
The beauteous spirits do engirt thee round,
White Iope, blithe Helen, and the rest,
To hear the stories of thy finish'd love
From that smooth tongue, whose music hell can move:

Then wilt thou speak of banqueting delights,
Of masks and revels which sweet youth did make,
Of tourneys and great challenges of knights,
And all these triumphs for thy beauty's sake.
When thou hast told these honours done to thee,
Then tell, Oh, tell how thou didst murder me.

THOMAS CAMPION

Where are all thy beauties now, all hearts enchaining?
Whither are thy flatterers gone with all their faining?
All fled; and thou alone still here remaining.

Thy rich state of twisted gold to baize is turned;
Cold as thou art, are thy loves that so much burned:
Who die in flatt'rers' arms are seldom mourned.

Yet, in spite of envy, this be still proclaimed,
That none worthier than thyself thy worth hath blamed:
When their poor names are lost, thou shalt live famed.

When thy story, long time hence, shall be perused,
Let the blemish of thy rule be thus excused:
None ever liv'd more just, none more abused.

THOMAS CAMPION

179 MY SILKS AND FINE ARRAY

My silks and fine array,
  My smiles and languish'd air,
By love are driv'n away;
  And mournful lean Despair
Brings me yew to deck my grave:
Such end true lovers have.

His face is fair and heav'n,
  When springing buds unfold;
O why to him was't giv'n,
  Whose heart is wintry cold?
His breast is love's all worship'd tomb,
Where all love's pilgrims come.

Bring me an axe and spade,
　Bring me a winding sheet;
When I my grave have made,
　Let winds and tempests beat:
Then down I'll lie, as cold as clay.
True love doth pass away!

WILLIAM BLAKE

180

The Queen of Paphos, Erycine,
In heart did rose-cheek'd Adon love,
He mortal was but she divine,
And oft with kisses did him move;
With great gifts still she did him woo,
But he would never yield thereto.

Then since the Queen of Love by Love
To love was once a subject made,
And could thereof no pleasure prove,
By day, by night, by light or shade,
Why being mortal should I grieve,
Since she herself could not relieve?

She was a goddess heavenly,
And lov'd a fair fac'd earthly boy,
Who did contemn her deity,
And would not grant her hope of joy,
For Love doth govern by a fate,
That here plants will, and there leaves hate.

But I a hapless mortal wight,
To an immortal beauty sue;

No marvel then she loathes my sight,
Since Adon Venus would not woo,
Hence, groaning sighs, mirth be my friend
Before my life, my love shall end.

ANON.

181 LIKE TO A HERMIT POOR

Like to a hermit poor in place obscure,
I mean to spend my days of endless doubt,
To wail such woes as time cannot recure,
Where none but Love shall ever find me out.

My food shall be of care and sorrow made,
My drink nought else but tears fall'n from mine eyes,
And for my light in such obscured shade,
The flames shall serve, which from my heart arise.

A gown of gray my body shall attire,
My staff of broken hope whereon I'll stay,
Of late repentance link'd with long desire
The couch is fram'd whereon my limbs I'll lay.

And at my gate Despair shall linger still,
To let in Death when Love and Fortune will.

? SIR WALTER RALEGH (from the French
of PHILIPPE DESPORTES)

O Love, Love, Love! O withering might!
O sun, that from thy noonday height
Shudderest when I strain my sight,
Throbbing thro' all thy heat and light,
   Lo, falling from my constant mind,
   Lo, parch'd and wither'd, deaf and blind,
   I whirl like leaves in roaring wind.

Last night I wasted hateful hours
Below the city's eastern towers:
I thirsted for the brooks, the showers:
I roll'd among the tender flowers:
   I crush'd them on my breast, my mouth;
   I look'd athwart the burning drouth
   Of that long desert to the south.

Last night, when some one spoke his name,
From my swift blood that went and came
A thousand little shafts of flame
Were shiver'd in my narrow frame.
   O Love, O fire! once he drew
   With one long kiss my whole soul thro'
   My lips, as sunlight drinketh dew.

Before he mounts the hill, I know
He cometh quickly: from below
Sweet gales, as from deep gardens, blow
Before him, striking on my brow.
   In my dry brain my spirit soon,
   Down-deepening from swoon to swoon,
   Faints like a dazzled morning moon.

The wind sounds like a silver wire,
And from beyond the noon a fire
Is pour'd upon the hills, and nigher
The skies stoop down in their desire;
   And, isled in sudden seas of light,
   My heart, pierced thro' with fierce delight,
   Bursts into blossom in his sight.

My whole soul waiting silently,
All naked in a sultry sky,
Droops blinded with his shining eye:
I *will* possess him or will die.
   I will grow round him in his place,
   Grow, live, die looking on his face,
   Die, dying clasp'd in his embrace.

ALFRED TENNYSON

183

My thoughts are winged with hopes, my hopes with love,
Mount, love, unto the moon in clearest night,
And say as she doth in the heavens move
In earth so wanes and waxeth my delight:
And whisper this but softly in her ears,
  Hope oft doth hang the head, and trust shed tears.

And you my thoughts that some mistrust do carry,
If for mistrust my mistress do you blame,
Say though you alter, yet you do not varry,
As she doth change, and yet remain the same:
Distrust doth enter hearts, but not infect,
  And love is sweetest seasoned with suspect.

If she for this, with clouds do mask her eyes,
And make the heavens dark with her disdain,
With windy sighs disperse them in the skies,
Or with thy tears dissolve them into rain;
Thoughts, hopes, and love return to me no more,
  Till Cynthia shine as she hath done before.

? SIR WALTER RALEGH

184　THE DEFINITION OF LOVE

My Love is of a birth as rare
As 'tis for object strange and high:
It was begotten by Despair
Upon Impossibility.

Magnanimous Despair alone
Could show me so divine a thing,
Where feeble Hope could ne'er have flown
But vainly flapped its tinsel wing.

And yet I quickly might arrive
Where my extended soul is fixt,
But Fate does iron wedges drive,
And always crowds itself betwixt.

For Fate with jealous eye does see
Two perfect Loves; nor lets them close:
Their union would her ruin be,
And her tyrannic power depose.

And therefore her decrees of steel
Us as the distant poles have placed,
(Though Love's whole world on us doth wheel)
Not by themselves to be embraced.

Unless the giddy heaven fall,
And earth some new convulsion tear;
And, us to join, the world should all
Be cramped into a planisphere.

As lines so Loves oblique may well
Themselves in every angle greet:
But ours so truly parallel,
Though infinite, can never meet.

Therefore the Love which us doth bind
But Fate so enviously debars,
Is the conjunction of the mind,
And opposition of the stars.

ANDREW MARVELL

185

My hopes retire; my wishes as before
Struggle to find their resting-place in vain:
The ebbing sea thus beats against the shore;
The shore repels it; it returns again.

WALTER SAVAGE LANDOR

186 SONG

MEDIOCRITY IN LOVE REJECTED

Give me more love or more disdain;
  The torrid or the frozen zone
Bring equal ease unto my pain,
  The temperate affords me none:
Either extreme of love or hate,
Is sweeter than a calm estate.

Give me a storm; if it be love,
　　Like Danaë in that golden shower,
I swim in pleasure; if it prove
　　Disdain, that torrent will devour
My vulture-hopes; and he's possess'd
Of heaven, that's but from hell released.
　　　　Then crown my joys or cure my pain:
　　　　Give me more love or more disdain.

THOMAS CAREW

187

You smiled, you spoke, and I believed,
By every word and smile deceived.
Another man would hope no more;
Nor hope I what I hoped before:
But let not this last wish be vain;
Deceive, deceive me once again!

WALTER SAVAGE LANDOR

188

And if I did what then?
Are you aggriev'd therefore?
The sea hath fish for every man,
And what would you have more?

Thus did my Mistress once,
Amaze my mind with doubt:
And popt a question for the nonce,
To beat my brains about.

Whereto I thus replied,
Each fisherman can wish,
That all the sea at every tide,
Were his alone to fish.

And so did I (in vain),
But since it may not be:
Let such fish there as find the gain,
And leave the loss for me.

And with such luck and loss,
I will content my self:
Till tides of turning time may toss,
Such fishers on the shelf.

And when they stick on sands,
That every man may see:
Then will I laugh and clap my hands,
As they do now at me.

GEORGE GASCOIGNE

189

Ring out your bells, let mourning shows be spread,
  For Love is dead:
    All Love is dead, infected
    With plague of deep disdain:
    Worth as nought worth rejected,
    And Faith fair scorn doth gain.
      From so ungrateful fancy,
      From such a female franzy,
      From them that use men thus,
      Good Lord deliver us.

Weep, neighbours, weep, do you not hear it said,
　　That Love is dead?
　　　　His death-bed, peacock's folly,
　　　　His winding-sheet is shame,
　　　　His will false-seeming holy,
　　　　His sole exec'tor blame.
　　　　　　From so ungrateful fancy,
　　　　　　From such a female franzy,
　　　　　　From them that use men thus,
　　　　　　Good Lord deliver us.

Let dirge be sung, and trentals rightly read,
　　For Love is dead:
　　　　Sir Wrong his tomb ordaineth,
　　　　My mistress' marble heart,
　　　　Which epitaph containeth,
　　　　'Her eyes were once his dart.'
　　　　　　From so ungrateful fancy,
　　　　　　From such a female franzy,
　　　　　　From them that use men thus,
　　　　　　Good Lord deliver us.

Alas, I lie: rage hath this error bred,
　　Love is not dead.
　　　　Love is not dead, but sleepeth
　　　　In her unmatched mind:
　　　　Where she his counsel keepeth,
　　　　Till due desert she find.
　　　　　　Therefore from so vile fancy,
　　　　　　To call such wit a franzy,
　　　　　　Who Love can temper thus,
　　　　　　Good Lord deliver us.

SIR PHILIP SIDNEY

190 SONG

I

Fire, fire,
 Is there no help for thy desire?
 Are tears all spent? is Humber low?
 Doth Trent stand still? doth Thames not flow?
 And does the Ocean backward go?
  Though all these can't thy fever cure,
   Yet Tyburn is a cooler lure,
 And since thou can'st not quench thy fire,
 Go hang thy self, and thy desire.

II

Fire, fire,
Here's one left for thy desire,
 Since that the rainbow in the sky,
 Is bent a deluge to deny,
 As loth for thee a God should lie,
  Let gentle rope come dangling down,
  One born to hang shall never drown,
And since thou can'st not quench the fire,
 Go hang thy self, and thy desire.

HENRY BOLD

4

LOVE CONTINUED

191 TO HELEN

Helen, thy beauty is to me
  Like those Nicean barks of yore,
That gently, o'er a perfumed sea,
  The weary, wayworn wanderer bore
  To his own native shore.

On desperate seas long wont to roam,
  Thy hyacinth hair, thy classic face,
Thy Naiad airs have brought me home
  To the glory that was Greece,
  To the grandeur that was Rome.

Lo! in yon brilliant window niche,
  How statue-like I see thee stand,
  The agate lamp within thy hand!
Ah, Psyche, from the regions which
  Are Holy Land!

EDGAR ALLAN POE

192 LOVE WHAT IT IS

Love is a circle that doth restless move
In the same sweet eternity of love.

ROBERT HERRICK

193

Like as a huntsman after weary chace,
  Seeing the game from him escapt away,
  Sits down to rest him in some shady place,
  With panting hounds beguiled of their prey:
So after long pursuit and vain assay,
  When I all weary had the chace forsook,
  The gentle dear return'd the selfsame way,
  Thinking to quench her thirst at the next brook:
There she beholding me with milder look,
  Sought not to fly, but fearless still did bide:
  Till I in hand her yet half trembling took,
  And with her own goodwill her firmly tied.
Strange thing meseem'd to see a beast so wild,
  So goodly won with her own will beguil'd.

EDMUND SPENSER

194 VERGIER

In orchard under the hawthorne
She has her lover till morn,
Till the traist man cry out to warn
Them. God, how swift the night,
                    And day comes on!

O Plasmatour, that thou end not the night,
Nor take my belovèd from my sight,
Nor I, nor tower-man, look on daylight,
'Fore God, how swift the night,
                    And day comes on!

'Lovely thou art, to hold me close and kisst,
Now cry the birds out, in the meadow mist,
Despite the cuckold, do thou as thou list,
So swiftly goes the night,
     And day comes on!

'My pretty boy, make we our play again
Here in the orchard where the birds complain,
'Till the traist watcher his song unrein,
Ah God! How swift the night,
     And day comes on!'

'Out of the wind that blows from her,
That dancing and gentle is and thereby pleasanter,
Have I drunk a draught, sweeter than scent of myrrh.
Ah God! How swift the night,
     And day comes on!'

Venust the lady, and none lovelier,
For her great beauty, many men look on her,
Out of my love will her heart not stir.
By God, how swift the night,
     And day comes on!

     EZRA POUND (from the Provençal)

195 ALBA

As cool as the pale wet leaves
     of lily-of-the-valley
She lay beside me in the dawn.

     EZRA POUND

196

The torch of Love dispels the gloom
Of life, and animates the tomb;
But never let it idly flare
On gazers in the open air,
Nor turn it quite away from one
To whom it serves for moon and sun,
And who alike in night or day
Without it could not find his way.

WALTER SAVAGE LANDOR

197

Fain would I change that note
To which fond love hath charmed me,
Long, long to sing by rote,
Fancying that that harmed me;
   Yet when this thought doth come
   Love is the perfect sum
      Of all delight.
   I have no other choice
   Either for pen or voice,
      To sing or write:

O Love, they wrong thee much,
That say thy sweet is bitter,
When thy ripe fruit is such
As nothing can be sweeter.
   Fair house of joy and bliss,
   Where truest pleasure is,

I do adore thee:
I know thee what thou art,
I serve thee with my heart,
And fall before thee.

ANON.

198 DUET

1. Is it the wind of the dawn that I hear
    in the pine overhead?
2. No; but the voice of the deep as it hollows
    the cliffs of the land.
1. Is there a voice coming up with the
    voice of the deep from the strand,
One coming up with a song in the
    flush of the glimmering red?
2. Love that is born of the deep coming
    up with the sun from the sea.
1. Love that can shape or can shatter a
    life till the life shall have fled?
2. Nay, let us welcome him, Love that
    can lift up a life from the dead.
1. Keep him away from the lone little isle.
    Let us be, let us be.
2. Nay, let him make it his own, let him
    reign in it—he, it is he,
Love that is born of the deep coming
    up with the sun from the sea.

ALFRED TENNYSON

199 IN KERRY

We heard the thrushes by the shore and sea,
And saw the golden stars' nativity,
Then round we went the lane by Thomas Flynn,
Across the church where bones lie out and in;
And there I asked beneath a lonely cloud
Of strange delight, with one bird singing loud,
What change you'd wrought in graveyard, rock and sea,
This new wild paradise to wake for me. . . .
Yet knew no more than knew these merry sins
Had built this stack of thigh-bones, jaws and shins.

J. M. SYNGE

200 FRONLEICHNAM

You have come your way, I have come my way;
You have stepped across your people, carelessly, hurting them all;
I have stepped across my people, and hurt them in spite of my care.

But steadily, surely, and notwithstanding
We have come our ways and met at last
Here in this upper room.

Here the balcony
Overhangs the street where the bullock-wagons slowly
Go by with their loads of green and silver birch-trees
For the feast of Corpus Christi.

Here from the balcony
We look over the growing wheat, where the jade-green river
Goes between the pine-woods,
Over and beyond to where the many mountains
Stand in their blueness, flashing with snow and the morning.

I have done; a quiver of exultation goes through me, like the first
Breeze of the morning through a narrow white birch.
You glow at last like the mountain tops when they catch
Day and make magic in heaven.
At last I can throw away world without end, and meet you
Unsheathed and naked and narrow and white;
At last you can throw immortality off, and I see you
Glistening with all the moment and all your beauty.

Shameless and callous I love you;
Out of indifference I love you;
Out of mockery we dance together,
Out of the sunshine into the shadow,
Passing across the shadow into the sunlight,
Out of sunlight to shadow.

As we dance
Your eyes take all of me in as a communication;
As we dance
I see you, ah, in full!
Only to dance together in triumph of being together
Two white ones, sharp, vindicated,
Shining and touching,
Is heaven of our own, sheer with repudiation

D. H. LAWRENCE

201 BIBLIOTHECA BODLEIANA

Edwardus Comes Clarendoniae
Clamped to his niche by an iron brace
Lifts to the white mercy of sparrows
His foppish foolish face.

Primus Angliae Cancellarius,
He's joined the race of stone.
I belong still to your race
Of warm mouth and bone.

Bibliotheca Bodleiana,
My library is love for a while.
O Illuminatio mea, I wait
For your entering smile.

GEOFFREY GRIGSON

202

On a time, the amorous Silvy,
Said to her Shepherd, Sweet how do you?
Kiss me this once, and then God be wi' you,
      My sweetest dear.
Kiss me this once, and then God be wi' you,
For now the morning draweth near.

With that her fairest bosom showing,
Opening her lips, rich perfumes blowing;
She said, Now kiss me and be going,
      My sweetest dear.
Kiss me this once and then be going,
For now the morning draweth near.

With that the Shepherd wak'd from sleeping,
And spying where the day was peeping,
He said, Now take my soul in keeping:
      My sweetest dear.
Kiss me, and take my soul in keeping,
Since I must go now, day is near.

ANON. (from the French)

203 CHANT DU CIEL

La fleur des Alpes disait au coquillage: « tu luis »
Le coquillage disait à la mer: « tu résonnes »
La mer disait au bateau: « tu trembles »
Le bateau disait au feu: « tu brilles »
Le feu me disait: « je brille moins que ses yeux »
Le bateau me disait: « je tremble moins que ton
cœur quand elle paraît »
La mer me disait: « je résonne moins que son nom
en ton amour »
Le coquillage me disait: « je luis moins que le phos-
phore du désir dans ton rêve creux »
La fleur des Alpes me disait: « elle est belle »
Je disait: « elle est belle, elle est belle, elle est émou-
vante »

ROBERT DESNOS

204 SHEPHERDESS

All day my sheep have mingled with yours. They strayed
Into your valley seeking a change of ground.
Held and bemused with what they and I had found,
Pastures and wonders, heedlessly I delayed.

Now it is late. The tracks leading home are steep,
The stars and landmarks in your country are strange.
How can I take my sheep back over the range?
Shepherdess, show me now where I may sleep.

NORMAN CAMERON

Come, come, my love, the bush is growing.
    The linnet sings the tune again
He sung when thou with garments flowing
    Went talking with me down the lane.
Dreaming of beauty ere I found thee,
    And musing by the bushes green;
The wind, enamoured, streaming round thee
    Painted the visions I had seen.

I guessed thy face without the knowing
    Was beautiful as e'er was seen;
I thought so by thy garments flowing
    And gait as airy as a queen;
Thy shape, thy size, could not deceive me:
    Beauty seemed hid in every limb;
And then thy face, when seen, believe me,
    Made every former fancy dim.

Yes, when thy face in beauty brightened
    The music of a voice divine,
Upon my heart thy sweetness lightened;
    Life, love, that moment, all were thine;
All I imagined musing lonely,
    When dreaming 'neath the greenwood tree,
Seeming to fancy visions only,
    Breathed living when I met with thee.

I wander oft, not to forget thee
    But just to feel those joys again.
When by the hawbush stile I met thee
    And heard thy voice adown the lane

Return me its good-humoured greeting:
   And oh, what music met my ear!
And then thy looks of wonder meeting,
   To see me come and talk so near!

Thy face that held no sort of scorning,
   Thy careless jump to reach the may;
That bush—I saw it many a morning
   And hoped to meet thee many a day;
Till winter came and stripped the bushes,
   The thistle withered on the moors,
Hopes sighed like winds along the rushes—
   I could not meet thee out of doors.

But winter's gone and spring is going
   And by thy own fireside I've been,
And told thee, dear, with garments flowing
   I met thee when the spring was green;
When travellers through snow-deserts rustle,
   Far from the strife of humankind,
How little seems the noise and bustle
   Of places they have left behind!

And on that long-remembered morning
   When first I lost this heart of mine,
Fame, all I'd hoped for, turned to scorning
   And love and hope lived wholly thine;
I told thee, and with rapture glowing
   I heard thee more than once declare,
That down the lane with garments flowing
   Thou with the spring wouldst wander there.

JOHN CLARE

Under the lime tree on the daisied ground
 Two that I know of made this bed.
There you may see heaped and scattered round
 Grass and blossoms broken and shed
  All in a thicket down in the dale;
Tandaradei—sweetly sang the nightingale.

Ere I set foot in the meadow already
 Some one was waiting for somebody;
There was a meeting—Oh! gracious lady,
 There is no pleasure again for me,
  Thousands of kisses there he took.
Tandaradei—see my lips, how red they look.

Leaf and blossom he had pulled and piled
 For a couch, a green one, soft and high;
And many a one hath gazed and smiled
 Passing the bower and pressed grass by;
  And the roses crushed hath seen,
Tandaradei—where I laid my head between.

In this love passage if any one had been there,
 How sad and shamed should I be;
But what were we adoing alone among the green there
 No soul shall ever know except my love and me,
  And the little nightingale,
Tandaradei—she, I wot, will tell no tale.

WALTHER VON DER VOGELWEIDE
(translated from the German by THOMAS LOVELL BEDDOES)

Strange fits of passion have I known:
　And I will dare to tell,
But in the Lover's ear alone,
　What once to me befell.

When she I loved looked every day
　Fresh as a rose in June,
I to her cottage bent my way,
　Beneath an evening-moon.

Upon the moon I fixed my eye,
　All over the wide lea;
With quickening pace my horse drew nigh
　Those paths so dear to me.

And now we reached the orchard-plot;
　And, as we climbed the hill,
The sinking moon to Lucy's cot
　Came near, and nearer still.

In one of those sweet dreams I slept,
　Kind Nature's gentlest boon!
And all the while my eyes I kept
　On the descending moon.

My horse moved on; hoof after hoof
　He raised, and never stopped:
When down behind the cottage roof,
　At once, the bright moon dropped.

What fond and wayward thoughts will slide
　Into a Lover's head!
'O mercy!' to myself I cried,
　'If Lucy should be dead!'

WILLIAM WORDSWORTH

208 THE QUESTION ANSWER'D

What is it men in women do require?
The lineaments of Gratified Desire.
What is it women do in men require?
The lineaments of Gratified Desire.

WILLIAM BLAKE

209

Abstinence sows sand all over
The ruddy limbs and flaming hair,
But Desire Gratified
Plants fruits of life and beauty there.

WILLIAM BLAKE

210 BRIDAL SONG

By female voices

We have bathed, where none have seen us,
   In the lake and in the fountain,
      Underneath the charmed statue
Of the timid, bending Venus,
   When the water-nymphs were counting
In the waves the stars of night,
      And those maidens started at you,
Your limbs shone through so soft and bright.
      But no secrets dare we tell,
         For thy slaves unlace thee,
         And he who shall embrace thee,
      Waits to try thy beauty's spell.

We have crowned thee queen of women,
  Since love's love, the rose, hath kept her
  Court within thy lips and blushes,
And thine eye, in beauty swimming,
  Kissing, rendered up the sceptre,
At whose touch the startled soul
  Like an ocean bounds and gushes,
And spirits bend at thy controul.
  But no secrets dare we tell,
    For thy slaves unlace thee,
    And he, who shall embrace thee,
  Is at hand, and so farewell.

THOMAS LOVELL BEDDOES

211 [*from* THE SONG OF SOLOMON]

I am the rose of Sharon, and the lily of the valleys. As the lily among thorns, so is my love among the daughters.

As the apple tree among the trees of the wood, so is my beloved among the sons. I sat down under his shadow with great delight, and his fruit was sweet to my taste. He brought me to the banqueting house, and his banner over me was love.

Stay me with flagons, comfort me with apples, for I am sick of love. His left hand is under my head, and his right hand doth embrace me. I charge you, O ye daughters of Jerusalem, by the roes, and by the hinds of the field, that ye stir not up, nor awake my love, till he please.

The voice of my beloved! behold, he cometh leaping upon the mountains, skipping upon the hills. My beloved is like a roe or a young hart: behold, he standeth behind our wall, he looketh forth at the windows, shewing himself through the lattice.

My beloved spake, and said unto me, Rise up, my love, my fair one, and come away. For, lo, the winter is past, the rain is over and gone. The flowers appear on the earth; the time of the singing of birds is come, and the voice of the turtle is heard in our land. The fig tree putteth forth her green figs, and the vines with the tender grape give a good smell. Arise, my love, my fair one, and come away.

O my dove that art in the clefts of the rock, in the secret places of the stairs, let me see thy countenance, let me hear thy voice; for sweet is thy voice, and thy countenance is comely. Take us the foxes, the little foxes, that spoil the vines: for our vines have tender grapes.

My beloved is mine, and I am his: he feedeth among the lilies. Until the day break, and the shadows flee away, turn, my beloved, and be thou like a roe or a young hart upon the mountains of Bether.

212

Je ne veux comparer tes beautez à la Lune:
La Lune est inconstante, et ton vouloir n'est qu'un.
Encor moins au Soleil: le Soleil est commun,
Commune est sa lumiere, et tu n'es pas commune.

Tu forces par vertu l'envie et la rancune.
Je ne suis, te louant, un flateur importun.
Tu sembles à toy-mesme, et n'as portrait aucun:
Tu es toute ton Dieu, ton Astre et ta Fortune.

Ceux qui font de leur Dame à toy comparaison,
Sont ou presomptueux, ou perclus de raison:
D'esprit et de sçavoir de bien loin tu les passes.

Ou bien quelque Demon de ton corps s'est vestu,
Ou bien tu es portrait de la mesme Vertu,
Ou bien tu es Pallas, ou bien l'une des Graces.

PIERRE DE RONSARD

What I fancy, I approve,
No dislike there is in love:
Be my Mistress short or tall,
And distorted therewithal:
Be she likewise one of those,
That an acre hath of nose:
Be her forehead, and her eyes
Full of incongruities:
Be her cheeks so shallow too,
As to shew her tongue wag through:
Be her lips ill hung, or set,
And her grinders black as jet;
Has she thin hair, hath she none,
She's to me a paragon.

ROBERT HERRICK

214

Ces longues nuicts d'hyver, où la Lune ocieuse
Tourne si lentement son char tout à l'entour,
Où le coq si tardif nous annonce le jour,
Où la nuict semble un an à l'ame soucieuse,

Je fusse mort d'ennuy sans ta forme douteuse,
Qui vient par une feinte alleger mon amour,
Et faisant toute nue entre mes bras sejour,
Me pipe doucement d'une joye menteuse.

Vraye tu es farouche, et fiere en cruauté.
De toy fausse on jouyst en toute privauté.
Pres ton mort je m'endors, pres de luy je repose:

Rien ne m'est refusé. Le bon sommeil ainsi
Abuse par le faux mon amoureux souci.
S'abuser en amour n'est pas mauvaise chose.

PIERRE DE RONSARD

Oh! I vu'st know'd o' my true love,
   As the bright moon up above,
Though her brightness wer my pleasure,
   She wer heedless o' my love.
Tho' 'twer all gaÿ to my eyes,
Where her feäir feäce did arise,
She noo mwore thought upon my thoughts,
   Than the high moon in the skies.

Oh! I vu'st heärd her a-zingen,
   As a sweet bird on a tree,
Though her zingen wer my pleasure,
   'Twer noo zong she zung to me.
Though her sweet vaïce that wer nigh,
Meäde my wild heart to beät high,
She noo mwore thought upon my thoughts,
   Than the birds would passers by.

Oh! I vu'st know'd her a-weepen,
   As a raïn-dimm'd mornen sky,
Though her tear-draps dimm'd her blushes,
   They wer noo draps I could dry.
Ev'ry bright tear that did roll,
Wer a keen païn to my soul,
But noo heart's pang she did then veel,
   Wer vor my words to console.

But the wold times be a-vanish'd,
   An' my true love is my bride,
An' her kind heart have a-meäde her
   As an angel at my zide;

I've her best smiles that mid plaÿ,
I've her me'th when she is gaÿ,
When her tear-draps be a-rollen,
    I can now wipe em awaÿ.

WILLIAM BARNES

216 NO PLATONIC LOVE

Tell me no more of minds embracing minds,
    And hearts exchang'd for hearts;
That spirits spirits meet, as winds do winds,
    And mix their subt'lest parts;
That two unbodied essences may kiss,
And then like angels, twist and feel one bliss.

I was that silly thing that once was wrought
    To practise this thin love;
I climb'd from sex to soul, from soul to thought;
    But thinking there to move,
Headlong I roll'd from thought to soul, and then
From soul I lighted at the sex agen.

As some strict down-look'd men pretend to fast,
    Who yet in closets eat;
So lovers who profess they spirits taste,
    Feed yet on grosser meat;
I know they boast they souls to souls convey,
Howe'er they meet, the body is the way.

Come, I will undeceive thee, they that tread
    Those vain aerial ways,
Are like young heirs and alchymists misled
    To waste their wealth and days,
For searching thus to be for ever rich,
They only find a med'cine for the itch.

WILLIAM CARTWRIGHT

217 MEETING AT NIGHT

I

The grey sea and the long black land;
And the yellow half-moon large and low;
And the startled little waves that leap
In fiery ringlets from their sleep,
As I gain the cove with pushing prow,
And quench its speed i' the slushy sand.

II

Then a mile of warm sea-scented beach;
Three fields to cross till a farm appears;
A tap at the pane, the quick sharp scratch
And blue spurt of a lighted match,
And a voice less loud, thro' its joys and fears,
Than the two hearts beating each to each!

ROBERT BROWNING

218 [*from* IN A GONDOLA]

She sings.

i

The moth's kiss first!
Kiss me as if you made believe
You were not sure, this eve,
How my face, your flower, had pursed
Its petals up; so, here and there
You brush it, till I grow aware
Who wants me, and wide ope I burst.

ii

The bee's kiss, now!
Kiss me as if you entered gay
My heart at some noonday,
A bud that dares not disallow
The claim, so all is rendered up,
And passively its shattered cup
Over your head to sleep I bow.

ROBERT BROWNING

219 GOING TO BED

Come, Madam, come, all rest my powers defy,
Until I labour, I in labour lie.
The foe oft-times having the foe in sight
Is tired with standing though he never fight.
Off with that girdle, like heaven's zone glittering,
But a far fairer world incompassing.
Unpin that spangled breastplate which you wear,
That th'eyes of busy fools may be stopt there.
Unlace yourself, for that harmonious chime
Tells me from you that now it is bed time.
Off with that happy busk, which I envie,
That still can be, and still can stand so nigh.
Your gown going off such beauteous state reveals
As when from flow'ry meads th'hill's shadow steals.
Off with that wiry coronet and show
The hairy diadem which on you doth grow:
Now off with those shoes, and then safely tread
In this love's hallow'd temple, this soft bed.
In such white robes, heaven's angels us'd to be
Receiv'd by men; thou angel bring'st with thee

A heaven like Mahomet's paradise; and though
Ill spirits walk in white, we easly know
By this these angels from an evil sprite,
Those set our hairs, but these our flesh upright.

License my roving hands, and let them go,
Before, behind, between, above, below.
O my America! my new-found-land,
My kingdom, safeliest when with one man mann'd,
My mine of precious stones, my emperie,
How blest am I in this discovering thee!
To enter in these bonds, is to be free;
Then where my hand is set, my seal shall be.

Full nakedness! All joys are due to thee,
As souls unbodied, bodies uncloth'd must be,
To taste whole joys. Gems which you women use
Are like Atlanta's balls, cast in men's views,
That when a fool's eye lighteth on a gem,
His earthly soul may covet theirs, not them.
Like pictures, or like books' gay coverings made
For lay-men, are all women thus array'd;
Themselves are mystic books, which only we
(Whom their imputed grace will dignify)
Must see reveal'd. Then since that I may know,
As liberally, as to a midwife, show
Thy self: cast all, yea, this white linen hence,
There is no penance due to innocence.

To teach thee, I am naked first; why then
What need'st thou have more covering than a man?

JOHN DONNE

220 THE VISITOR

She brings that breath, and music too,
   That comes when April's days begin;
And sweetness Autumn never had
   In any bursting skin.

She's big with laughter at the breasts,
   Like netted fish they leap:
Oh God, that I were far from here,
   Or lying fast asleep!

W. H. DAVIES

221 TO HIS LOVE

Come away, come, sweet love,
The golden morning breaks,
All the earth, all the air
Of love and pleasure speaks,
Teach thine arms then to embrace,
And sweet rosy lips to kiss,
And mix our souls in mutual bliss.
Eyes were made for beauty's grace,
Viewing, rueing love's long pain,
Procur'd by beauty's rude disdain.

Come away, come, sweet love,
The golden morning wastes,
While the sun from his sphere
His fiery arrows casts:
Making all the shadows fly,
Playing, staying in the grove,

To entertain the stealth of love,
Thither, sweet love, let us hie,
Flying, dying, in desire,
Wing'd with sweet hopes and heav'nly fire.

Come away, come, sweet love,
Do not in vain adorn
Beauty's grace that should rise
Like to the naked morn:
Lilies on the river's side,
And fair Cyprian flowers new blown,
Desire no beauties but their own,
Ornament is nurse of pride,
Pleasure, measure, love's delight,
Haste then, sweet love, our wished flight.

ANON.

222 [*from* TROILUS AND CRESSIDA]

Her bed is India; there she lies, a pearl.

WILLIAM SHAKESPEARE

223 [*from* ROMEO AND JULIET]

i

(*Enter Juliet alone: she speaks*)

Gallop apace, you fiery-footed steeds,
Towards Phoebus' lodging! Such a wagoner
As Phaeton would whip you to the west
And bring in cloudy night immediately.
Spread thy close curtain, love-performing night,

That runaways' eyes may wink, and Romeo
Leap to these arms untalked of and unseen.
Lovers can see to do their amorous rites
By their own beauties; or, if love be blind,
It best agrees with night. Come, civil night,
Thou sober-suited matron, all in black,
And learn me how to lose a winning match,
Played for a pair of stainless maidenhoods.
Hood my unmanned blood, bating in my cheeks,
With thy black mantle till strange love grow bold,
Think true love acted simple modesty.
Come, night; come, Romeo; come, thou day in night;
For thou wilt lie upon the wings of night
Whiter than new snow upon a raven's back,
Come, gentle night; come, loving, black-browed night;
Give me my Romeo; and, when he shall die,
Take him and cut him out in little stars,
And he will make the face of heaven so fine
That all the world will be in love with night
And pay no worship to the garish sun.
O, I have bought the mansion of a love,
But not possessed it; and though I am sold,
Not yet enjoyed. So tedious is this day
As is the night before some festival
To an impatient child that hath new robes
And may not wear them. O, here comes my nurse,
And she brings news; and every tongue that speaks
But Romeo's name speaks heavenly eloquence.

ii

(*Enter Romeo and Juliet aloft*)

JULIET
     Wilt thou be gone? It is not yet near day.
     It was the nightingale, and not the lark,

That pierced the fearful hollow of thine ear.
Nightly she sings on yond pomegranate tree.
Believe me, love, it was the nightingale.

ROMEO

It was the lark, the herald of the morn;
No nightingale. Look, love, what envious streaks
Do lace the severing clouds in yonder East.
Night's candles are burnt out, and jocund day
Stands tiptoe on the misty mountain tops.
I must be gone and live, or stay and die.

JULIET

Yond light is not daylight; I know it, I.
It is some meteor that the sun exhales
To be to thee this night a torchbearer
And light thee on thy way to Mantua.
Therefore stay yet; thou need'st not to be gone.

ROMEO

Let me be ta'en, let me be put to death.
I am content, so thou wilt have it so,
I'll say yon grey is not the morning's eye,
'Tis but the pale reflex of Cynthia's brow;
Nor that is not the lark whose notes do beat
The vaulty heaven so high above our heads.
I have more care to stay than will to go.
Come, death, and welcome! Juliet wills it so.
How is't, my soul? Let's talk; it is not day.

JULIET

It is, it is! Hie hence, be gone, away!
It is the lark that sings so out of tune,
Straining harsh discords and unpleasing sharps.
Some say the lark makes sweet division;
This doth not so, for she divideth us.
Some say the lark and loathèd toad change eyes;
O, now I would they had changed voices too,
Since arm from arm that voice doth us affray,

Hunting thee hence with hunt's-up to the day.
O, now be gone! More light and light it grows.

ROMEO

More light and light—more dark and dark our woes.

WILLIAM SHAKESPEARE

224

And is it night? Are they thine eyes that shine?
　Are we alone and here and here alone?
May I come near, may I but touch thy shrine?
　Is Jealousy asleep, and is he gone?
O Gods, no more, silence my lips with thine,
　Lips, kisses, joys, hap, blessings most divine.

O come, my dear, our griefs are turn'd to night,
　And night to joys, night blinds pale Envy's eyes,
Silence and sleep prepare us our delight,
　O cease we then our woes, our griefs, our cries,
O vanish words, words do but passions move,
　O dearest life, joys sweet, O sweetest love.

ANON.

225

Now sleeps the crimson petal, now the white;
Nor waves the cypress in the palace walk;
Nor winks the gold fin in the porphyry font.
The fire-fly wakens; waken thou with me.

Now droops the milk-white peacock like a ghost,
And like a ghost she glimmers on to me.

Now lies the Earth all Danaë to the stars,
And all thy heart lies open unto me.

Now slides the silent meteor on, and leaves
A shining furrow, as thy thoughts in me.

Now folds the lily all her sweetness up,
And slips into the bosom of the lake:
So fold thyself, my dearest, thou, and slip
Into my bosom and be lost in me.

ALFRED TENNYSON

226 LES ROSES DE SAADI

J'ai voulu, ce matin, te rapporter des roses;
Mais j'en avais tant pris dans mes ceintures closes
Que les nœuds trop serrés n'ont pu les contenir.

Les nœuds ont éclaté. Les roses envolées
Dans le vent, à la mer s'en sont toutes allées.
Elles ont suivi l'eau pour ne plus revenir.

La vague en a paru rouge et comme enflammée:
Ce soir ma robe encore en est tout embaumée:
Respires-en sur moi l'odorant souvenir.

MARCELINE DESBORDES-VALMORE

All night by the rose, rose,
　　All night by the rose I lay;
Dared I not the rose steal,
　　And yet I bare the flower away.

ANON.

228　A SONG

Ask me no more where Jove bestows,
When June is past, the fading rose;
For in your beauty's orient deep
These flowers, as in their causes, sleep.

Ask me no more whither do stray
The golden atoms of the day;
For in pure love heaven did prepare
Those powders to enrich your hair.

Ask me no more whither doth haste
The nightingale, when May is past;
For in your sweet dividing throat
She winters, and keeps warm her note.

Ask me no more where those stars 'light,
That downwards fall in dead of night;
For in your eyes they sit, and there
Fixed become, as in their sphere.

Ask me no more if east or west
The phœnix builds her spicy nest;
For unto you at last she flies,
And in your fragrant bosom dies.

THOMAS CAREW

229 ΕΡΟΣ Δ'ΑΥΤΕ ...

Crimson nor yellow roses, nor
The savour of the mounting sea
Are worth the perfume I adore
That clings to thee.

The languid-headed lilies tire,
The changeless waters weary me.
I ache with passionate desire
Of thine and thee.

There are but these things in the world—
Thy mouth of fire,
Thy breasts, thy hands, thy hair upcurled,
And my desire!

THEODORE WRATISLAW

230 STANCES

Quand au temple nous serons
Agenouillez, nous ferons
Les devots selon la guise
De ceux qui pour loüer Dieu
Humbles se courbent au lieu
Le plus secret de l'Eglise.
Mais quand au lict nous serons
Entrelassez, nous ferons
Les lascifs selon les guises
Des Amans qui librement
Pratiquent folastrement
Dans les draps cent mignardises.
Pourquoy donque, quand je veux
Ou mordre tes beaux cheveux,

Ou baiser ta bouche aimée,
Ou toucher à ton beau sein,
Contrefais-tu la nonnain
Dedans un cloistre enfermée?

Pour qui gardes-tu tes yeux
Et ton sein delicieux,
Ton front, ta lévre jumelle?
En veux-tu baiser Pluton
Là bas, apres que Charon
T'aura mise en sa nacelle?

Apres ton dernier trespas,
Gresle, tu n'auras là bas
Qu'une bouchette blesmie;
Et quand mort je te verrois
Aux Ombres je n'avou'rois
Que jadis tu fus m'amie.

Ton test n'aura plus de peau,
Ny ton visage si beau
N'aura veines ny arteres:
Tu n'auras plus que les dents
Telles qu'on les voit dedans
Les testes de cimeteres.

Donque tandis que tu vis,
Change, Maistresse, d'avis,
Et ne m'espargne ta bouche.
Incontinent tu mourras,
Lors tu te repentiras
De m'avoir esté farouche.

Ah, je meurs! ah, baise moy!
Ah, Maistresse, approche toy!
Tu fuis comme un fan qui tremble.
Au-moins souffre que ma main
S'esbate un peu dans ton sein,
Ou plus bas, si bon te semble.

PIERRE DE RONSARD

231 [THE FACE THAT LAUNCHED A THOUSAND SHIPS, *from* DOCTOR FAUSTUS]

(Doctor Faustus speaks)

Was this the face that launched a thousand ships?
And burnt the topless towers of Ilium?
Sweet Helen, make me immortal with a kiss:
Her lips suck forth my soul, see where it flies:
And all is dross that is not Helena:
I will be Paris, and for love of thee,
Instead of Troy shall Wertenberg be sack'd,
And I will combat with weak Menelaus,
And wear thy colours on my plumed crest:
Yea I will wound Achillis in the heel,
And then return to Helen for a kiss.
O thou art fairer than the evening air,
Clad in the beauty of a thousand stars,
Brighter art thou than flaming Jupiter,
When he appear'd to hapless Semele,
More lovely than the monarch of the sky
In wanton Arethusa's azur'd arms,
And none but thou shalt be my paramour.

CHRISTOPHER MARLOWE

232 CORINNAE CONCUBITUS

In summer's heat and mid-time of the day
To rest my limbs upon a bed I lay,
One window shut, the other open stood,
Which gave such light as twinkles in a wood,
Like twilight glimpse at setting of the sun
Or night being past, and yet not day begun.

Such light to shamefaced maidens must be shown,
Where they may sport, and seem to be unknown.
Then came Corinna in a long loose gown,
Her white neck hid with tresses hanging down:
Resembling fair Semiramis going to bed
Or Lais of a thousand wooers sped.
I snatched her gown, being thin, the harm was small,
Yet strived she to be covered therewithal.
And striving thus as one that would be cast,
Betrayed herself, and yielded at the last.
Stark naked as she stood before mine eye,
Not one wen in her body could I spy.
What arms and shoulders did I touch and see,
How apt her breasts were to be pressed by me!
How smooth a belly under her waist saw I!
How large a leg, and what a lusty thigh!
To leave the rest, all liked me passing well,
I clinged her naked body, down she fell,
Judge you the rest: being tired she bad me kiss,
Jove send me more such afternoons as this.

CHRISTOPHER MARLOWE
(from the Latin of OVID)

233 LES BIJOUX

La très-chère était nue, et, connaissant mon cœur,
Elle n'avait gardé que ses bijoux sonores,
Dont le riche attirail lui donnait l'air vainqueur
Qu'ont dans leurs jours heureux les esclaves des Mores.

Quand il jette en dansant son bruit vif et moqueur,
Ce monde rayonnant de métal et de pierre
Me ravit en extase, et j'aime à la fureur
Les choses où le son se mêle à la lumière.

Elle était donc couchée et se laissait aimer,
Et du haut du divan elle souriait d'aise
À mon amour profond et doux comme la mer,
Qui vers elle montait comme vers sa falaise.

Les yeux fixés sur moi, comme un tigre dompté,
D'un air vague et rêveur elle essayait des poses,
Et la candeur unie à la lubricité
Donnait un charme neuf à ses métamorphoses;

Et son bras et sa jambe, et sa cuisse et ses reins,
Polis comme de l'huile, onduleux comme un cygne,
Passaient devant mes yeux clairvoyants et sereins;
Et son ventre et ses seins, ces grappes de ma vigne,

S'avançaient, plus câlins que les Anges du mal,
Pour troubler le repos où mon âme était mise,
Et pour la déranger du rocher de cristal
Où, calme et solitaire, elle s'était assise.

Je croyais voir unis par un nouveau dessin
Les hanches de l'Antiope au buste d'un imberbe,
Tant sa taille faisait ressortir son bassin.
Sur ce teint fauve et brun le fard était superbe!

— Et la lampe s'étant résignée à mourir,
Comme le foyer seul illuminait la chambre,
Chaque fois qu'il poussait un flamboyant soupir,
Il inondait de sang cette peau couleur d'ambre!

CHARLES BAUDELAIRE

234 WITH A GIFT OF RINGS

It was no costume jewellery I sent:
True stones cool to the tongue, their settings ancient,
Their magic evident.
Conceal your pride, accept them negligently
But, naked on your couch, wear them for me.

ROBERT GRAVES

235 LE PARFUM

Lecteur, as-tu quelquefois respiré
Avec ivresse et lente gourmandise
Ce grain d'encens qui remplit une église,
Ou d'un sachet le musc invétéré?

Charme profond, magique, dont nous grise
Dans le présent le passé restauré!
Ainsi l'amant sur un corps adoré
Du souvenir cueille la fleur exquise.

De ses cheveux élastiques et lourds,
Vivant sachet, encensoir de l'alcôve,
Une senteur montait, sauvage et fauve,

Et des habits, mousseline ou velours,
Tout imprégnés de sa jeunesse pure,
Se dégageait un parfum de fourrure.

CHARLES BAUDELAIRE

236 RIDDLE

Their tongues are knives, their forks are hands and feet.
They feed each other through their skins and eat
Religiously the spiced, symbolic meat.
The loving oven cooks them in its heat—
Two curried lovers on a rice-white sheet.

ADRIAN MITCHELL

237 CALYPSO'S SONG TO ULYSSES

My hands are tender feathers,
They can teach your body to soar.
My feet are two comedians
With jokes your flesh has never heard before.

So try to read the meaning
Of the blue veins under my skin
And feel my breasts like gentle wheels
Revolving from your thighs to your chin.

And listen to the rhythm
Of my heartbeat marking the pace
And see the visions sail across
The easy-riding waters of my face.

What is sweeter than the human body?
Two human bodies as they rise and fall.
What is sweeter than two loving bodies?
There is nothing sweeter at all.
Lose yourself, find yourself,
Lose yourself again
On the island of Calypso.

ADRIAN MITCHELL

238 [*from* TRILOGY FOR X]

And love hung still as crystal over the bed
  And filled the corners of the enormous room;
The boom of dawn that left her sleeping, showing
  The flowers mirrored in the mahogany table.

O my love, if only I were able
  To protract this hour of quiet after passion,
Not ration happiness but keep this door for ever
  Closed on the world, its own world closed within it.

But dawn's waves trouble with the bubbling minute,
  The names of books come clear upon their shelves,
The reason delves for duty and you will wake
  With a start and go on living on your own.

The first train passes and the windows groan,
  Voices will hector and your voice become
A drum in tune with theirs, which all last night
  Like sap that fingered through a hungry tree
Asserted our one night's identity.

LOUIS MACNEICE

239 RIVER ROSES

By the Isar, in the twilight
We were wandering and singing,
By the Isar, in the evening
We climbed the huntsman's ladder and sat swinging
In the fir-tree overlooking the marshes,
While river met with river, and the ringing

Of their pale-green glacier water filled the evening.
By the Isar, in the twilight
We found the dark wild roses
Hanging red at the river; and simmering
Frogs were singing, and over the river closes
Was savour of ice and of roses; and glimmering
Fear was abroad. We whispered: 'No one knows us.
Let it be as the snake disposes
Here in this simmering marsh.'

D. H. LAWRENCE

240 ON THE BALCONY

In front of the sombre mountains, a faint, lost ribbon of rainbow;
And between us and it, the thunder;
And down below in the green wheat, the labourers
Stand like dark stumps, still in the green wheat.

You are near to me, and your naked feet in their sandals,
And through the scent of the balcony's naked timber
I distinguish the scent of your hair: so now the limber
Lightning falls from heaven.

Adown the pale-green glacier river floats
A dark boat through the gloom—and whither?
The thunder roars. But still we have each other!
The naked lightnings in the heavens dither
And disappear—what have we but each other?
The boat has gone.

D. H. LAWRENCE

241 GREEN

The dawn was apple-green,
   The sky was green wine held up in the sun,
The moon was a golden petal between.

She opened her eyes, and green
   They shone, clear like flowers undone
For the first time, now for the first time seen.

D. H. LAWRENCE

242 GLOIRE DE DIJON

When she rises in the morning
I linger to watch her;
She spreads the bath-cloth underneath the window
And the sunbeams catch her
Glistening white on the shoulders,
While down her sides the mellow
Golden shadow glows as
She stoops to the sponge, and her swung breasts
Sway like full-blown yellow
Gloire de Dijon roses.

She drips herself with water, and her shoulders
Glisten as silver, they crumple up
Like wet and falling roses, and I listen
For the sluicing of their rain-dishevelled petals.
In the window full of sunlight
Concentrates her golden shadow
Fold on fold, until it glows as
Mellow as the glory roses.

D. H. LAWRENCE

243 THE SUN RISING

Busy old fool, unruly Sun,
Why dost thou thus,
Through windows, and through curtains call on us?
Must to thy motions lovers' seasons run?
Saucy pedantic wretch, go chide
Late school-boys, and sour 'prentices,
Go tell court-huntsmen that the King will ride,
Call country ants to harvest offices;
Love, all alike, no season knows, nor clime,
Nor hours, days, months, which are the rags of time.

Thy beams, so reverend, and strong
Why shouldst thou think?
I could eclipse and cloud them with a wink,
But that I would not lose her sight so long:
If her eyes have not blinded thine,
Look, and tomorrow late, tell me,
Whether both the Indias of spice and mine
Be where thou left'st them, or lie here with me.
Ask for those kings whom thou saw'st yesterday,
And thou shalt hear, 'All here in one bed lay.'

She is all States, and all Princes, I;
Nothing else is.
Princes do but play us; compar'd to this,
All honour's mimic; all wealth alchemy.
Thou Sun art half as happy as we,
In that the world's contracted thus;
Thine age asks ease, and since thy duties be
To warm the world, that's done in warming us.
Shine here to us, and thou art every where;
This bed thy centre is, these walls, thy sphere.

JOHN DONNE

Puisque j'ai mis ma lèvre à ta coupe encor pleine,
Puisque j'as dans tes mains posé mon front pâli,
Puisque j'ai respiré parfois la douce haleine
De ton âme, parfum dans l'ombre enseveli;

Puisqu'il me fut donné de t'entendre me dire
Les mots où se répand le cœur mystérieux,
Puisque j'ai vu pleurer, puisque j'ai vu sourire
Ta bouche sur ma bouche et tes yeux sur mes yeux;

Puisque j'ai vu briller sur ma tête ravie
Un rayon de ton astre, hélas! voilé toujours,
Puisque j'ai vu tomber dans l'onde de ma vie
Une feuille de rose arrachée à tes jours,

Je puis maintenant dire aux rapides années:
— Passez! passez toujours! je n'ai plus à vieillir!
Allez-vous-en avecs vos fleurs toutes fanées;
J'ai dans l'âme une fleur que nul ne peut cueillir!

Votre aile en le heurtant ne fera rien répandre
Du vase où je m'abreuve et que j'ai bien rempli.
Mon âme a plus de feu que vous n'avez de cendre!
Mon cœur a plus d'amour que vous n'avez d'oubli!

Ier janvier 1835. Minuit et demi.

VICTOR HUGO

245 [TO HIS MISTRESS]

So swete a kis yistrene fra thee I reft,
In bowing down thy body on the bed,
That evin my lyfe within thy lippis I left;
Sensyne from thee my spirit wald never shed.

To folow thee it from my body fled,
And left my corps als cold as ony kie.
Bot, when the danger of my death I dred,
To seik my spreit I sent my harte to thee;
Bot it wes so inamored with thyn ee,
With thee it myndit likwyse to remane:
So thou hes keepit captive all the thrie,
More glaid to byde then to returne agane.
Except thy breath thare places had suppleit,
Even in thyn armes thair, doutles, had I deit.

ALEXANDER MONTGOMERIE

246 A PASTORAL DIALOGUE

SHEPHERD. NYMPH. CHORUS.

SHEPHERD. This mossy bank they press'd. NYMPH. That aged oak
 Did canopy the happy pair
 All night from the damp air.
CHORUS. Here let us sit and sing the words they spoke,
Till the day breaking, their embraces broke.

SHEPHERD. See, love, the blushes of the morn appear,
 And now she hangs her pearly store
 (Robb'd from the Eastern shore)
I'th'cowslip's bell, and roses rare:
Sweet, I must stay no longer here.

NYMPH. Those streaks of doubtful light usher not day,
 But show my sun must set; no morn
 Shall shine till thou return,
The yellow planets, and the gray
Dawn, shall attend thee on thy way.

SHEPHERD. If thine eyes gild my paths, they may forbear
    Their useless shine.   NYMPH. My tears will quite
  Extinguish their faint light.
SHEPHERD. Those drops will make their beams more clear,
Love's flames will shine in every tear.

CHORUS. They kiss'd, and wept, and from their lips, and eyes,
    In a mix'd dew of briny sweet,
  Their joys and sorrows meet.
But she cries out.   NYMPH. Shepherd, arise,
The sun betrays us else to spies.

SHEPHERD. The winged hours fly fast, whilst we embrace,
    But when we want their help to meet,
  They move with leaden feet.
NYMPH. Then let us pinion Time, and chase
The day for ever from this place.

SHEPHERD. Hark! NYMPH. Ay me, stay! SHEPHERD. For ever.
    NYMPH. No, arise,
  We must be gone.   SHEPHERD. My nest of spice.
   NYMPH. My soul.   SHEPHERD. My Paradise.
CHORUS. Neither could say farewell, but through their eyes
Grief interrupted speech with tears' supplies.

THOMAS CAREW

247 TO CYNTHIA

ON HER EMBRACES

If thou a reason dost desire to know,
My dearest Cynthia, why I love thee so,
As when I do enjoy all thy love's store,
I am not yet content, but seek for more;

When we do kiss so often as the tale
Of kisses doth outvie the winter's hail:
When I do print them on more close and sweet
Than shells of scollops, cockles when they meet,
Yet am not satisfied: when I do close
Thee nearer to me than the ivy grows
Unto the oak: when those white arms of thine
Clip me more close than doth the elm the vine:
When naked both, thou seemest not to be
Contiguous, but continuous parts of me:
And we in bodies are together brought
So near, our souls may know each other's thought
Without a whisper: yet I do aspire
To come more close to thee, and to be higher.
No, 'twas well said, that spirits are too high
For bodies, when they meet, to satisfy;
Our souls having like forms of light and sense,
Proceeding from the same intelligence,
Desire to mix like to two water drops,
Whose union some little hindrance stops,
Which meeting both together would be one.
For in the steel, and in the adamant stone,
One and the same magnetic soul is cause,
That with such unseen chains each other draws:
So our souls now divided, brooked not well,
That being one, they should asunder dwell.
Then let me die, that so my soul being free,
May join with that her other half in thee,
For when in thy pure self it shall abide,
It shall assume a body glorified,
Being in that high bliss; nor shall we twain
Or wish to meet, or fear to part again.

SIR FRANCIS KYNASTON

When I heard at the close of the day how my name had been
receiv'd with plaudits in the capitol, still it was not a happy night
for me that follow'd,

And else when I carous'd, or when my plans were accomplish'd,
still I was not happy,

But the day when I rose at dawn from the bed of perfect health,
refresh'd, singing, inhaling the ripe breath of autumn,

When I saw the full moon in the west grow pale and disappear in
the morning light,

When I wander'd alone over the beach, and undressing bathed,
laughing with the cool waters, and saw the sun rise,

And when I thought how my dear friend my lover was on his way
coming, O then I was happy,

O then each breath tasted sweeter, and all that day my food nourish'd
me more, and the beautiful day pass'd well,

And the next came with equal joy, and with the next at evening
came my friend,

And that night while all was still I heard the waters roll slowly
continually up the shores,

I heard the hissing rustle of the liquid and sands as directed to me
whispering to congratulate me,

For the one I love most lay sleeping by me under the same cover in
the cool night,

In the stillness in the autumn moonbeams his face was inclined
toward me,

And his arm lay lightly around my breast—and that night I was
happy.

WALT WHITMAN

249 SOMETIMES WITH ONE I LOVE

Sometimes with one I love I fill myself with rage for fear I effuse
    unreturn'd love,
But now I think there is no unreturn'd love, the pay is certain one
    way or another,
(I loved a certain person ardently and my love was not return'd,
Yet out of that I have written these songs.)

WALT WHITMAN

250 THE LOVER SHOWETH HOW HE IS FORSAKEN OF SUCH AS HE SOMETIME ENJOYED

They flee from me that sometime did me seek
With naked foot stalking in my chamber.
I have seen them gentle, tame and meek,
That now are wild and do not remember
That sometime they put themself in danger
To take bread at my hand; and now they range,
Busily seeking with a continual change.

Thanked be fortune, it hath been otherwise
Twenty times better; but once in special,
In thin array after a pleasant guise,
When her loose gown from her shoulders did fall,
And she me caught in her arms long and small;
Therewithal sweetly did me kiss,
And softly said, Dear heart, how like you this?

It was no dream: I lay broad waking,
But all is turned thorough my gentleness
Into a strange fashion of forsaking;

And I have leave to go of her goodness,
And she also to use newfangleness.
But since that I so kindely am served,
I would fain know what she hath deserved.

SIR THOMAS WYATT

251

My true love hath my heart, and I have his,
By just exchange one for another given.
I hold his dear, and mine he cannot miss:
There never was a better bargain driven.
My true love hath my heart and I have his.

His heart in me, keeps him and me in one,
My heart in him, his thoughts and senses guides:
He loves my heart, for once it was his own:
I cherish his, because in me it bides.
My true love hath my heart and I have his.

SIR PHILIP SIDNEY

252   PART OF PLENTY

When she carries food to the table and stoops down
—Doing this out of love—and lays soup with its good
Tickling smell, or fry winking from the fire
And I look up, perhaps from a book I am reading
Or other work: there is an importance of beauty
Which can't be accounted for by there and then,
And attacks me, but not separately from the welcome
Of the food, or the grace of her arms.

When she puts a sheaf of tulips in a jug
And pours in water and presses to one side
The upright stems and leaves that you hear creak,
Or loosens them, or holds them up to show me,
So that I see the tangle of their necks and cups
With the curls of her hair, and the body they are held
Against, and the stalk of the small waist rising
And flowering in the shape of breasts;
Whether in the bringing of the flowers or of the food
She offers plenty, and is part of plenty,
And whether I see her stooping, or leaning with the flowers,
What she does is ages old, and she is not simply,
No, but lovely in that way.

BERNARD SPENCER

253   TWO ARE TOGETHER

Two are together, I tell you,
A slope of a voel, are a corner;
Grass short as a garden,
Bracken
Uncoiling,
Foxgloves, water
Descending,
Quartz in a stone.

This corner:
Mountain-ash (ferns
Up in air).
Then over an edge
This single
Blue wedge of a mountain;
This comfort, you tell me,
Contentment,
Compassion.

This wild-mint-scented scene
And wild roses
And wrinkle of water descending
Tending to laughter;
Together, then
After.

GEOFFREY GRIGSON

254

Let me not to the marriage of true minds
Admit impediments, love is not love
Which alters when it alteration finds,
Or bends with the remover to remove.
O no! it is an ever-fixed mark,
That looks on tempests and is never shaken;
It is the star to every wand'ring bark,
Whose worth's unknown, although his height be taken.
Love's not Time's fool, though rosy lips and cheeks
Within his bending sickle's compass come,
Love alters not with his brief hours and weeks,
But bears it out even to the edge of doom:
  If this be error and upon me proved,
  I never writ, nor no man ever loved.

WILLIAM SHAKESPEARE

255 COUNTING THE BEATS

You, love, and I,
(He whispers) you and I,
And if no more than only you and I
What care you or I?

Counting the beats,
Counting the slow heart beats,
The bleeding to death of time in slow heart beats,
Wakeful they lie.

Cloudless day,
Night, and a cloudless day;
Yet the huge storm will burst upon their heads one day
From a bitter sky.

Where shall we be,
(She whispers) where shall we be,
When death strikes home, O where then shall we be
Who were you and I?

Not there but here,
(He whispers) only here,
As we are, here, together, now and here,
Always you and I.

Counting the beats,
Counting the slow heart beats,
The bleeding to death of time in slow heart beats,
Wakeful they lie.

ROBERT GRAVES

256

So well I love thee, as without thee I
Love nothing; if I might choose, I'd rather die
Than be one day debarr'd thy company.

Since beasts, and plants do grow, and live and move,
Beasts are those men, that such a life approve:
He only lives, that deadly is in love.

The corn that in the ground is sown first dies
And of one seed do many ears arise:
Love, this world's corn, by dying multiplies.

The seeds of love first by thy eyes were thrown
Into a ground untill'd, a heart unknown
To bear such fruit, till by thy hands 'twas sown.

Look as your looking-glass by chance may fall,
Divide and break in many pieces small
And yet shows forth the selfsame face in all:

Proportions, features, graces just the same,
And in the smallest piece as well the name
Of fairest one deserves, as in the richest frame.

So all my thoughts are pieces but of you
Which put together makes a glass so true
As I therein no other's face but yours can view.

MICHAEL DRAYTON

257

Sleep now, O sleep now,
    O you unquiet heart!
A voice crying 'Sleep now'
    Is heard in my heart.

The voice of the winter
    Is heard at the door.
O sleep, for the winter
    Is crying 'Sleep no more'.

My kiss will give peace now
   And quiet to your heart—
Sleep on in peace now,
   O you unquiet heart!

JAMES JOYCE

258 WINTER WINDS COLD AND BLEA

Winter winds cold and blea
Chilly blows o'er the lea:
Wander not out to me,
   Jenny so fair,
Wait in thy cottage free.
   I will be there.

Wait in thy cushioned chair
Wi' thy white bosom bare.
Kisses are sweetest there:
   Leave it for me.
Free from the chilly air
   I will meet thee.

How sweet can courting prove,
How can I kiss my love
Muffled in hat and glove
   From the chill air?
Quaking beneath the grove,
   What love is there!

Lay by thy woollen vest,
Drape no cloak o'er thy breast:
Where my hand oft hath pressed,

Pin nothing there:
Where my head droops to rest,
Leave its bed bare.

JOHN CLARE

259

Weep you no more, sad fountains,
What need you flow so fast,
Look how the snowy mountains
Heav'n's sun doth gently waste.
But my sun's heav'nly eyes
View not your weeping,
That now lies sleeping
Softly now softly lies sleeping.

Sleep is a reconciling,
A rest that peace begets:
Doth not the sun rise smiling,
When fair at ev'n he sets?
Rest you, then rest, sad eyes,
Melt not in weeping,
While she lies sleeping
Softly now softly lies sleeping.

ANON.

260 CASHEL OF MUNSTER
IRISH RUSTIC BALLAD

I'd wed you without herds, without money, or rich array,
And I'd wed you on a dewy morning at day-dawn grey;
My bitter woe it is, love, that we are not far away
In Cashel town, though the bare deal board were our marriage-
bed this day;

Oh, fair maid, remember the green hill side,
Remember how I hunted about the valleys wide;
Time now, has worn me; my locks are turn'd to grey,
The year is scarce and I am poor, but send me not, love, away!

Oh, deem not my blood is of base strain, my girl,
Oh, deem not my birth was as the birth of the churl;
Marry me, and prove me, and say soon you will,
That noble blood is written on my right side still!

My purse holds no red gold, no coin of the silver white,
No herds are mine to drive through the long twilight!
But the pretty girl that would take me, all bare though I be and lone
Oh, I'd take her with me kindly to the county Tyrone.

Oh, my girl, I can see 'tis in trouble you are,
And, oh, my girl, I see 'tis your people's reproach you bear:
'I am a girl in trouble for his sake with whom I fly,
And, oh, may no other maiden know such reproach as I!'

SIR SAMUEL FERGUSON

261

O sweetheart, hear you
   Your lover's tale;
A man shall have sorrow
   When friends him fail.

For he shall know then
   Friends be untrue
And a little ashes
   Their words come to.

But one unto him
  Will softly move
And softly woo him
  In ways of love.

His hand is under
  Her smooth round breast;
So he who has sorrow
  Shall have rest.

JAMES JOYCE

262 ALONE

Nothing will fill the salt caves our youth wore:
Happiness later nor a house with corn
Ripe to its walls and open door.
We filtered through to sky and flowed into
A pit full of stars; so we are each alone.
Even in this being alone I meet with you.

E. J. SCOVELL

263

To me, fair friend, you never can be old,
For as you were when first your eye I eyed,
Such seems your beauty still: Three winters cold,
Have from the forests shook three summers' pride;
Three beauteous springs to yellow autumn turned,
In process of the seasons have I seen,
Three April perfumes in three hot Junes burned,
Since first I saw you fresh which yet are green.

Ah! yet doth beauty, like a dial-hand,
Steal from his figure, and no pace perceived;
So your sweet hue, which methinks still doth stand,
Hath motion, and mine eye may be deceived.
 For fear of which, hear this, thou age unbred,
 Ere you were born was beauty's summer dead.

WILLIAM SHAKESPEARE

264

When to the sessions of sweet silent thought,
I summon up remembrance of things past,
I sigh the lack of many a thing I sought,
And with old woes new wail my dear time's waste:
Then can I drown an eye (unus'd to flow)
For precious friends hid in death's dateless night,
And weep afresh love's long-since cancell'd woe,
And moan th' expense of many a vanish'd sight:
Then can I grieve at grievances foregone,
And heavily from woe to woe tell o'er
The sad account of fore-bemoaned moan,
Which I new pay as if not paid before.
 But if the while I think on thee (dear friend)
 All losses are restor'd, and sorrows end.

WILLIAM SHAKESPEARE

265

 Take heed of loving me;
At least remember I forbade it thee;
Not that I shall repair my unthrifty waste
 Of breath and blood, upon thy sighs and tears,

By being to thee then what to me thou wast;
  But so great joy our life at once outwears.
Then, lest thy love by my death frustrate be,
If thou love me, take heed of loving me.

  Take heed of hating me,
Or too much triumph in the victory;
Not that I shall be mine own officer,
  And hate with hate again retaliate;
But thou wilt lose the style of conqueror,
  If I, thy conquest, perish by thy hate.
Then, lest my being nothing lessen thee,
If thou hate me, take heed of hating me.

  Yet, love and hate me too;
So these extremes shall neither's office do;
Love me, that I may die the gentler way:
  Hate me, because thy love is too great for me;
Or let these two, themselves, not me, decay;
  So shall I live thy stage, not triumph be.
Lest thou thy love and hate and me undo,
To let me live, oh, love and hate me too!

JOHN DONNE

266 SONG

I

Chloris, forbear a while,
  Do not o'er joy me,
Urge not another smile
  Lest it destroy me.

That beauty pleases most,
    And is best taking,
Which soon is won, soon lost,
    Kind, yet forsaking,
I love a coming lady, faith! I do!
But now and then, I'd have her scornful too.

2

O'er cloud those eyes of thine,
    Bo-peep thy features,
Warm with an April shine,
    Scorch not thy creatures:
      Still to display thy ware,
      Still to be fooling,
      Argues how rude you are
      In Cupid's schooling.
Disdain begets a suit, scorn draws us nigh,
'Tis cause I would, and cannot, makes me try.

3

Fairest, I'd have thee wise,
    When gallants view thee,
And court, do thou despise;
    Fly, they'll pursue thee,
      Fasts move an appetite,
      Make hunger greater;
      Who's stinted of delight
      Falls to 't the better,
Be kind and coy by turns, be calm and rough!
And buckle now and then, and that's enough.

HENRY BOLD

5

ABSENCES, DOUBTS, DIVISION

267 [LADY MY TREASURE]

O my thoughts' sweet food, my, my only owner,
  O my heavens for taste by thy heavenly pleasure,
O the fair nymph born to do women honour,
                Lady my Treasure.

Where be now those joys, that I lately tasted?
  Where be now those eyes ever inly persers?
Where be now those words never idly wasted,
                Wounds to rehearsers?

Where is ah that face, that a sun defaces?
  Where be those welcomes by no worth deserved?
Where be those movings, the delights, the graces?
                How be we swerved?

O hideous absence, by thee am I thralled.
  O my vain word gone, ruin of my glory.
O due allegiance, by thee am I called
                Still to be sorry.

But no more words, though a word be spoken,
  Nor no more wording with a word to spill me.
Peace, due allegiance, duty must be broken,
                If duty kill me.

Then come, O come, then I do come, receive me,
  Slay me not, for stay do not hide thy blisses,
But between those arms, never else do leave me;
                Give me thy kisses.

O my thoughts' sweet food, my, my only owner,
  O my heavens for taste, by thy heavenly pleasure,
O the fair nymph born to do women honour,
                          Lady my Treasure.

SIR PHILIP SIDNEY

268 SONG: HOW CAN I CARE?

How can I care whether you sigh for me
  While still I sleep alone swallowing back
The spittle of desire, unmanned, a tree
  Pollarded of its crown, a dusty sack
  Tossed on the stable rack?

How can I care what coloured frocks you wear,
  What humming-birds you watch on jungle hills,
What phosphorescence wavers in your hair,
  Or with what water-music the night fills—
  Dear love, how can I care?

ROBERT GRAVES

269 ECHO

Come to me in the silence of the night;
  Come in the speaking silence of a dream;
Come with soft rounded cheeks and eyes as bright
  As sunlight on a stream;
    Come back in tears,
O memory, hope, love of finished years.

O dream how sweet, too sweet, too bitter sweet,
  Whose wakening should have been in Paradise,
Where souls brimfull of love abide and meet;
  Where thirsting longing eyes
    Watch the slow door
That opening, letting in, lets out no more.

Yet come to me in dreams, that I may live
  My very life again though cold in death:
Come back to me in dreams, that I may give
  Pulse for pulse, breath for breath:
    Speak low, lean low,
As long ago, my love, how long ago.

  18 *December* 1854.

CHRISTINA ROSSETTI

270 ABSENCES AND THE WIND

i

Blow, northern wynd,
Send thou me my sweeting,
Blow, northern wynd,
Blow, blow, blow.

ANON.

ii

Westron wynd, when will thou blow,
The small rain down can rain?
Christ, if my love were in my arms,
And I in my bed again.

ANON.

Is it no dream that I am he
    Whom one awake all night
Rose ere the earliest birds to see,
    And met by dawn's red light;

Who, when the wintry lamps were spent
    And all was drear and dark,
Against the rugged pear-tree leant
    While ice crackt off the bark;

Who little heeded sleet and blast,
    But much the falling snow;
Those in few hours would sure be past,
    His traces *that* might show;

Between whose knees, unseen, unheard,
    The honest mastiff came,
Nor fear'd he; no, nor was he fear'd:
    Tell me, am I the same?

O come! the same dull stars we'll see,
    The same o'er-clouded moon.
O come! and tell me am I he?
    O tell me, tell me soon.

WALTER SAVAGE LANDOR

272 COMPLAINT OF THE ABSENCE OF HER LOVER BEING UPON THE SEA

O happy dames, that may embrace
    The fruit of your delight,
Help to bewail the woeful case,
    And eke the heavy plight

Of me, that wonted to rejoice
The fortune of my pleasant choice;
Good ladies, help to fill my mourning voice.

In ship, freight with rememberance
  Of thoughts, and pleasures past,
He sails that hath in governance
  My life, while it will last;
With scalding sighs, for lack of gale,
Furthering his hope, that is his sail,
Toward me, the sweet port of his avail.

Alas how oft in dreams I see
  Those eyes, that were my food;
Which sometime so delighted me,
  That yet they do me good;
Wherewith I wake with his return,
Whose absent flame did make me burn:
But when I find the lack, Lord, how I mourn!

When other lovers in arms across
  Rejoice their chief delight,
Drowned in tears, to mourn my loss
  I stand the bitter night
In my window, where I may see
Before the winds how the clouds flee.
Lo, what a mariner love hath made me.

And in green waves when the salt flood
  Doth rise, by rage of wind,
A thousand fancies in that mood
  Assail my restless mind.
Alas, now drencheth my sweet foe,
That with the spoil of my heart did go,
And left me; but, alas, why did he so?

And when the seas wax calm again,
   To chase fro me annoy,
My doubtful hope doth cause me plain;
   So dread cuts off my joy.
Thus is my wealth mingled with woe,
And of each thought a doubt doth grow;
Now he comes, will he come? Alas, no no.

HENRY HOWARD, EARL OF SURREY

273 THE LADY PRAYETH THE RETURN
OF HER LOVER ABIDING ON THE SEAS

Shall I thus ever long, and be no whit the near,
And shall I still complain to thee, the which me will not hear?
Alas say nay, say nay, and be no more so dumb,
But open thou thy manly mouth, and say that thou wilt come;
Whereby my heart may think, although I see not thee,
That thou wilt come, thy word so sware, if thou a livesman be.

The roaring hugey waves, they threaten my poor ghost,
And toss thee up and down the seas, in danger to be lost.
Shall they not make me fear that they have swallowed thee?
But as thou art most sure alive so wilt thou come to me;
Whereby I shall go see thy ship ride on the strand
And think and say, Lo where he comes, and sure here will he land.

And then I shall lift up to thee my little hand,
And thou shalt think thine heart in ease, in health to see me stand.
And if thou come indeed (as Christ thee send to do),
Those arms that miss thee now shall then embrace thee too.
Each vein to every joint the lively blood shall spread,
Which now for want of thy glad sight doth show full pale and dead.

But if thou slip thy troth and do not come at all,
As minutes in the clock do strike so call for death I shall:
To please both thy false heart, and rid myself from woe,
That rather had to die in troth than live forsaken so.

ANON.

274

Like as the Culver on the bared bough,
   Sits mourning for the absence of her mate:
   And in her songs sends many a wishful vow,
   For his return that seems to linguer late:
So I alone now left disconsolate,
   Mourn to myself the absence of my love:
   And wand'ring here and there all desolate,
   Seek with my plaints to match that mournful dove:
Ne joy of aught that under heaven doth hove,
   Can comfort me, but her own joyous sight:
Whose sweet aspect both God and man can move,
   In her unspotted pleausance to delight.
Dark is my day, whiles her fair light I miss,
   And dead my life that wants such lively bliss.

EDMUND SPENSER

275 TO ALTHEA, FROM PRISON

   When Love with unconfined wings
      Hovers within my gates;
   And my divine Althea brings
      To whisper at the grates;

When I lie tangled in her hair,
  And fettered to her eye;
The Gods that wanton in the air
  Know no such liberty.

When flowing cups run swiftly round
  With no allaying Thames,
Our careless heads with roses bound
  Our hearts with loyal flames;
When thirsty grief in wine we steep,
  When healths and draughts go free,
Fishes that tipple in the deep
  Know no such liberty.

When, like committed linnets, I
  With shriller throat shall sing
The sweetness, mercy, majesty,
  And glories of my King;
When I shall voice aloud how good
  He is, how great should be,
Enlarged winds that curl the flood
  Know no such liberty.

Stone walls do not a prison make,
  Nor iron bars a cage;
Minds innocent and quiet take
  That for an hermitage;
If I have freedom in my love,
  And in my soul am free;
Angels alone that soar above
  Enjoy such liberty.

RICHARD LOVELACE

276

Constant Penelope sends to thee, careless Ulysses.
Write not again, but come, sweet mate, thy self to revive me.
Troy we do much envy, we desolate lost ladies of Greece,
Not Priamus, nor yet all Troy can us recompense make.
O that he had, when he first took shipping to Lacedaemon,
That adulter I mean, had been o'erwhelmed with waters.
Then I had not lain now all alone, thus quivering for cold,
Nor used this complaint, nor have thought the day to be so long.

ANON. (from the Latin of OVID)

277 AS IF A PHANTOM CARESS'D ME

As if a phantom caress'd me,
I thought I was not alone walking here by the shore;
But the one I thought was with me as now I walk by the shore,
   the one I loved that caress'd me,
As I lean and look through the glimmering light, that one
   has utterly disappear'd,
And those appear that are hateful to me and mock me.

WALT WHITMAN

278 ELEGY ON HIS MISTRESS

By our first strange and fatal interview,
By all desires which thereof did ensue,
By our long starving hopes, by that remorse
Which my words' masculine persuasive force

Begot in thee, and by the memory
Of hurts which spies and rivals threatened me,
I calmly beg: But by thy parents' wrath,
By all pains, which want and divorcement hath,
I conjure thee; and all the oaths which I
And thou have sworn, to seal joint constancy,
Here I unswear, and overswear them thus;
Thou shalt not love by means so dangerous.
Temper, O fair Love, love's impetuous rage,
Be my true mistress still, not my feigned page.
I'll go, and, by thy kind leave, leave behind
Thee, only worthy to nurse in my mind
Thirst to come back; O if thou die before,
From other lands my soul towards thee shall soar.
Thy (else almighty) beauty cannot move
Rage from the seas, nor thy love teach them love,
Nor tame wild Boreas' harshness; thou hast read
How roughly he in pieces shivered
Fair Orithea, whom he swore he lov'd.
Fall ill or good, 'tis madness to have prov'd
Dangers unurg'd; feed on this flattery,
That absent lovers one in the other be.
Dissemble nothing, not a boy, nor change
Thy body's habit, nor mind's; be not strange
To thyself only; all will spy in thy face
A blushing womanly discovering grace;
Richly cloth'd apes are call'd apes, and as soon
Eclips'd as bright we call the moon the moon.
Men of France, changeable chameleons,
Spittles of diseases, shops of fashions,
Love's fuellers, and the rightest company
Of players, which upon the world's stage be,
Will quickly know thee, and no less, alas!
The indifferent Italian, as we pass
His warm land, well content to think thee page,

Will haunt thee, with such lust and hideous rage
As Lot's fair guests were vext. But none of these,
Nor spongy hydroptic Dutch, shall thee displease,
If thou stay here. O stay here; for, for thee
England is only a worthy gallery,
To walk in expectation, till from thence
Our greatest King call thee into his presence.
When I am gone, dream me some happiness;
Nor let thy looks our long-hid love confess,
Nor praise, nor dispraise me, nor bless nor curse
Openly love's force, nor in bed fright thy nurse
With midnight's startings, crying out, Oh, Oh,
Nurse, O my love is slain; I saw him go
O'er the white Alps alone; I saw him, ay,
Assail'd, fight, taken, stabb'd, bleed, fall, and die.
Augur me better chance, except dread Jove
Think it enough for me to have had thy love.

JOHN DONNE

279 TO LUCASTA,
GOING TO THE WARS

I

Tell me not (Sweet) I am unkind,
    That from the nunnery
Of thy chaste breast, and quiet mind,
    To war and arms I fly.

II

True; a new mistress now I chase,
    The first foe in the field;
And with a stronger faith embrace
    A sword, a horse, a shield.

III

Yet this inconstancy is such,
    As you too shall adore;
I could not love thee (Dear) so much,
    Lov'd I not honour more.

RICHARD LOVELACE

280 A SONG

Absent from thee, I languish still;
    Then ask me not, when I return?
The straying fool 'twill plainly kill
    To wish all day, all night to mourn.

Dear! from thine arms then let me fly,
    That my fantastic mind may prove
The torments it deserves to try
    That tears my fixed heart from my love.

When, wearied with a world of woe,
    To thy safe bosom I retire
Where love and peace and truth does flow,
    May I contented there expire,

Lest, once more wandering from that heaven,
    I fall on some base heart unblest,
Faithless to thee, false, unforgiven,
    And lose my everlasting rest.

JOHN WILMOT, EARL OF ROCHESTER

281 AUPRÈS DE MA BLONDE

(FOLKSONG)

Dans le jardin d' mon père
Les lauriers sont fleuris,
Dans le jardin d' mon père
Les lauriers sont fleuris,
Tous les oiseaux du monde
Y vien't s'y rafraîchir
Auprès de ma blonde
Qu'il fait bon, fait bon, fait bon,
Auprès de ma blonde
Qu'il fait bon dormir.

Tous les oiseaux du monde
Y vienn't s'y rafraîchir,
La caill', la tourterelle
Et la joli' perdrix.

La caill', la tourterelle
Et la joli' perdrix'
Et ma joli' colombe
Qui chante jour et nuit.

Et ma joli' colombe
Qui chante jour et nuit,
Qui chante pour les filles
Qui n'ont pas de mari.

Qui chante pour les filles
Qui n'ont pas de mari.
Ne chante pas pour elle
Elle en a un joli.

Ne chante pas pour elle
Elle en a un joli.
Il est dans la Hollande,
Les Hollandais l'ont pris!

Il est dans la Hollande,
Les Hollandais l'ont pris!
— Que donn'rez vous, la belle,
A qui vou l'ira qu'ri?

— Que donn'rez vous, la belle,
A qui vou l'ira qu'ri?
— Je donnerai Touraine,
Paris et Saint-Denis.

— Je donnerai Touraine,
Paris et Saint-Denis,
La tour de Babylone,
Le clocher d' mon pays.

La tour de Babylone,
Le clocher d' mon pays,
Et ma joli' colombe
Qui chante jour et nuit.

282

As Love and I, late harbour'd in one inn,
With proverbs thus each other entertain:
In love there is no lack, thus I begin,
Fair words make fools, replieth he again;
Who spares to speak, doth spare to speed (quoth I),
As well (saith he) too forward, as too slow;
Fortune assists the boldest, I reply,
A hasty man (quoth he) ne'er wanted woe;

Labour is light, where love (quoth I) doth pay,
(Saith he) light burthen's heavy, if far born;
(Quoth I) the main lost, cast the bye away;
You have spun a fair thread, he replies in scorn.
    And having thus awhile each other thwarted,
    Fools as we met, so fools again we parted.

MICHAEL DRAYTON

283

Th'expense of spirit in a waste of shame
Is lust in action, and till action, lust
Is perjur'd, murd'rous, bloody, full of blame,
Savage, extreme, rude, cruel, not to trust;
Enjoy'd no sooner but despised straight;
Past reason hunted, and no sooner had,
Past reason hated as a swallowed bait,
On purpose laid to make the taker mad;
Mad in pursuit and in possession so;
Had, having, and in quest, to have, extreme;
A bliss in proof, and prov'd, a very woe;
Before a joy propos'd, behind a dream,
    All this the world well knows yet none knows well;
    To shun the heaven that leads men to this hell.

WILLIAM SHAKESPEARE

284

What meaneth this? When I lie alone,
I toss, I turn, I sigh, I groan;
My bed me seems as hard as stone:
        What means this?

I sigh, I plain continually;
The clothes that on my bed do lie
Always methinks they lie awry:
    What means this?

In slumbers oft for fear I quake;
For heat and cold I burn and shake;
For lack of sleep my head doth ache:
    What means this?

A-mornings then when I do rise
I turn unto my wonted guise;
All day after muse and devise
    What means this?

And if perchance by me there pass
She unto whom I sue for grace,
The cold blood forsaketh my face:
    What means this?

But if I sit near her by,
With loud voice my heart doth cry,
And yet my mouth is dumb and dry:
    What means this?

To ask for help no heart I have,
My tongue doth fail what I should crave,
Yet inwardly I rage and rave:
    What means this?

Thus have I passed many a year
And many a day, tho naught appear;
But most of that that I most fear:
    What means this?

SIR THOMAS WYATT

I

We have met late—it is too late to meet,
  O friend, not more than friend!
Death's forecome shroud is tangled round my feet,
And if I step or stir, I touch the end.
  In this last jeopardy
Can I approach thee, I, who cannot move?
How shall I answer thy request for love?
  Look in my face and see.

II

I love thee not, I dare not love thee! go
  In silence; drop my hand.
If thou seek roses, seek them where they blow
In garden-alleys, not in desert-sand.
  Can life and death agree,
That thou shouldst stoop thy song to my complaint?
I cannot love thee. If the word is faint,
  Look in my face and see.

III

I might have loved thee in some former days,
  Oh, then, my spirits had leapt
As now they sink, at hearing thy love-praise.
Before these faded cheeks were overwept,
  Had this been asked of me,
To love thee with my whole strong heart and head,—
I should have said still . . . yes, but *smiled* and said,
  'Look in my face and see!'

IV

But now . . . God sees me, God, who took my heart
   And drowned it in life's surge.
In all your wide warm earth I have no part—
A light song overcomes me like a dirge.
   Could Love's great harmony
The saints keep step to when their bonds are loose,
Not weigh me down? am *I* a wife to choose?
   Look in my face and see.

V

While I behold, as plain as one who dreams,
   Some woman of full worth,
Whose voice, as cadenced as a silver stream's,
Shall prove the fountain-soul which sends it forth;
   One younger, more thought-free
And fair and gay, than I, thou must forget,
With brighter eyes than these . . which are not wet . .
   Look in my face and see!

VI

So farewell thou, whom I have known too late
   To let thee come so near.
Be counted happy while men call thee great,
And one belovèd woman feels thee dear!—
   Not I!—that cannot be.
I am lost, I am changed,—I must go farther, where
The change shall take me worse, and no one dare
   Look in my face to see.

VII

Meantime I bless thee. By these thoughts of mine
   I bless thee from all such!

I bless thy lamp to oil, thy cup to wine,
Thy hearth to joy, thy hand to an equal touch
   Of loyal troth. For me,
I love thee not, I love thee not!—away!
Here's no more courage in my soul to say
   'Look in my face and see.'

ELIZABETH BARRETT BROWNING

286

When in disgrace with fortune and men's eyes,
I all alone beweep my out-cast state,
And trouble deaf heaven with my bootless cries,
And look upon myself, and curse my fate,
Wishing me like to one more rich in hope,
Featur'd like him, like him with friends possess'd,
Desiring this man's art, and that man's scope,
With what I most enjoy contented least,
Yet in these thoughts my self almost despising,
Haply I think on thee, and then my state,
(Like to the lark at break of day arising)
From sullen earth, sing's hymns at heaven's gate;
   For thy sweet love remember'red such wealth brings,
   That then I scorn to change my state with kings.

WILLIAM SHAKESPEARE

287 YOUTH AND BEAUTY

Thou art so fair, and young withal,
   Thou kindl'st young desires in me,
Restoring life to leaves that fall,
   And sight to eyes that hardly see
   Half those fresh beauties bloom in thee.

Those, under sev'ral herbs and flow'rs
  Disguis'd, were all Medea gave,
When she recall'd time's flying hours,
  And aged Aeson from his grave,
  For beauty can both kill and save.

Youth it enflames, but age it cheers,
  I would go back, but not return
To twenty but to twice those years;
  Not blaze, but ever constant burn,
  For fear my cradle prove my urn.

AURELIAN TOWNSEND

288 A SONG OF A YOUNG LADY TO HER ANCIENT LOVER

Ancient person, for whom I
All the flattering youth defy,
Long be it ere thou grow old,
Aching, shaking, crazy, cold;
  But still continue as thou art,
  Ancient person of my heart.

On thy withered lips and dry,
Which like barren furrows lie,
Brooding kisses I will pour
Shall thy youthful heat restore
(Such kind showers in autumn fall,
And a second spring recall);
  Nor from thee will ever part,
  Ancient person of my heart.

Thy nobler part, which but to name
In our sex would be counted shame,
By age's frozen grasp possessed,
From his ice shall be released,
And soothed by my reviving hand,
In former warmth and vigor stand.
All a lover's wish can reach
For thy joy my love shall teach,
And for thy pleasure shall improve
All that art can add to love.
    Yet still I love thee without art,
    Ancient person of my heart.

JOHN WILMOT, EARL OF ROCHESTER

289

Is it possible
That so high debate,
So sharp, so sore, and of such rate,
Should end so soon and was begone so late?
Is it possible?

Is it possible
So cruel intent,
So hasty heat and so soon spent,
From love to hate, and thence for to relent?
Is it possible?

Is it possible
That any may find
Within one heart so diverse mind,
To change or turn as weather and wind?
Is it possible?

Is it possible
To spy it in an eye
That turns as oft as chance on die?
The truth whereof can any try?
Is it possible?

It is possible
For to turn so oft,
To bring that lowest that was most aloft,
And to fall highest yet to light soft:
It is possible.

All is possible,
Who so list believe;
Trust therefore first, and after preve:
As men wed ladies by licence and leave,
All is possible.

SIR THOMAS WYATT

290 A WELL-WISHING TO A PLACE OF
PLEASURE

See the building
Where whilst my mistress lived in
  Was pleasure's essence,
See how it droopeth
And how nakedly it looketh
  Without her presence:
Every creature
That appertains to nature
  'Bout this house living,
Doth resemble,
If not dissemble,
  Due praises giving.

Hark, how the hollow
Winds do blow
   And seem to murmur
   In every corner
   For her long absence:
The which doth plainly show
The cause why I do now
All this grief and sorrow show.

See the garden
Where I receiv'd reward in
   For my true love:
Behold those places
Where I receiv'd those graces
   The Gods might move.
The Queen of plenty
With all the fruits are dainty,
   Delights to please,
Flora springing
Is ever bringing
   Dame Venus ease.
Oh see the arbour where that she
   With melting kisses
   Distilling blisses
From her true self
   With joy did ravish me.
The pretty nightingale
   Did sing melodiously.

Hail to those groves
Where I enjoy'd those loves
   So many days.
Let the flowers be springing,
And sweet birds ever singing
   Their roundelays,

Many Cupid's measures
And cause for true love's pleasures
  Be danc'd around,
Let all contentment
For mirth's presentment
  This day be found:
And may the grass grow ever green
  Where we two lying
  Have oft been trying
More several ways
  Than beauty's lovely Queen
When she in bed with Mars
  By all the gods was seen.

ANON.

291

Retired this hour from wondering crowds
And flower-fed poets swathed in clouds,
Now the dull dust is blown away,
Ianthe, list to what I say.
Verse is not always sure to please
For lightness, readiness, and ease;
Romantic ladies like it not
Unless its steams are strong and hot
As Melton-Mowbray stables when
Ill-favored frost comes back again.
Tell me no more you feel a pride
To be for ever at my side,
To think your beauty will be read
When all who pine for it are dead.
I hate a pomp and a parade
Of what should ever rest in shade;

What not the slenderest ray should reach,
Nor whispered breath of guarded speech:
There even Memory should sit
Absorbed, and almost doubting it.

WALTER SAVAGE LANDOR

292

Art thou afraid the adorer's prayer
  Be overheard? that fear resign.
He waves the incense with such care
  It leaves no stain upon the shrine.

WALTER SAVAGE LANDOR

293 SÉRÉNADE

Comme la voix d'un mort qui chanterait
  Du fond de sa fosse,
Maîtresse, entends monter vers ton retrait
  Ma voix aigre et fausse.

Ouvre ton âme et ton oreille au son
  De ma mandoline:
Pour toi j'ai fait, pour toi, cette chanson
  Cruelle et câline.

Je chanterai tes yeux d'or et d'onyx
  Purs de toutes ombres,
Puis le Léthé de ton sein, puis le Styx
  De tes cheveux sombres.

Comme la voix d'un mort qui chanterait
    Du fond de sa fosse,
Maîtresse, entends monter vers ton retrait
    Ma voix aigre et fausse.

Puis je louerai beaucoup, comme il convient,
    Cette chair bénie
Dont le parfum opulent me revient
    Les nuits d'insomnie.

Et pour finir je dirai le baiser,
    De ta lèvre rouge,
Et ta douceur à me martyriser,
    — Mon Ange! — ma Gouge!

Ouvre ton âme et ton oreille au son
    De ma mandoline:
Pour toi j'ai fait, pour toi, cette chanson
    Cruelle et câline.

PAUL VERLAINE

294 NON SUM QUALIS ERAM BONAE
SUB REGNO CYNARAE

Last night, ah, yesternight, betwixt her lips and mine
There fell thy shadow, Cynara! thy breath was shed
Upon my soul between the kisses and the wine;
And I was desolate and sick of an old passion,
    Yea, I was desolate and bowed my head:
I have been faithful to thee, Cynara! in my fashion.

All night upon mine heart I felt her warm heart beat,
Night-long within mine arms in love and sleep she lay;

Surely the kisses of her bought red mouth were sweet;
But I was desolate and sick of an old passion,
　　When I awoke and found the dawn was gray:
I have been faithful to thee, Cynara! in my fashion.

I have forgot much, Cynara! gone with the wind,
Flung roses, roses riotously with the throng,
Dancing, to put thy pale, lost lilies out of mine;
But I was desolate and sick of an old passion,
　　Yea, all the time, because the dance was long:
I have been faithful to thee, Cynara! in my fashion.

I cried for madder music and for stronger wine,
But when the feast is finished and the lamps expire,
Then falls thy shadow, Cynara! the night is thine;
And I am desolate and sick of an old passion,
　　Yea hungry for the lips of my desire:
I have been faithful to thee, Cynara! in my fashion.

ERNEST DOWSON

295

An evil spirit, your beauty haunts me still,
Wherewith (alas) I have been long possess'd,
Which ceaseth not to tempt me to each ill,
Nor gives me once, but one poor minute's rest:
In me it speaks, whether I sleep or wake,
And when by means, to drive it out I try,
With greater torments then it me doth take,
And tortures me in most extremity;
Before my face, it lays down my despairs,
And hastes me on unto a sudden death;
Now tempting me, to drown myself in tears,
And then in sighing, to give up my breath;

Thus am I still provok'd to every evil,
By this good wicked spirit, sweet angel devil.

MICHAEL DRAYTON

296 NO ONE SO MUCH AS YOU

No one so much as you
Loves this my clay,
Or would lament as you
Its dying day.

You know me through and through
Though I have not told,
And though with what you know
You are not bold.

None ever was so fair
As I thought you:
Not a word can I bear
Spoken against you.

All that I ever did
For you seemed coarse
Compared with what I hid
Nor put in force.

My eyes scarce dare meet you
Lest they should prove
I but respond to you
And do not love.

We look and understand,
We cannot speak
Except in trifles and
Words the most weak.

For I at most accept
Your love, regretting
That is all: I have kept
Only a fretting

That I could not return
All that you gave
And could not ever burn
With the love you have,

Till sometimes it did seem
Better it were
Never to see you more
Than linger here

With only gratitude
Instead of love—
A pine in solitude
Cradling a dove.

EDWARD THOMAS

297　THE OLD STORY

The old story is true of charms fading;
He knew her first before her charm was mellow—
Slim; surprise in her eyes; like a woodland creature
Crept abroad who found the world amazing,

Who, afterwards maturing, yet was dainty,
Light on her feet and gentle with her fingers;
Put on a little flesh, became an easy
Spreadeagled beauty for Renaissance painters.

And then she went; he did not see her after
Until by the shore of a cold sea in winter
With years behind her and the waves behind her.
Drubbing the memory up and down the pebbles.

Flotsam and wrack; the bag of old emotions;
Watch in the swirl her ten years back reflections—
White as a drowning hand, then gone for ever;
Here she stands who was twenty and is thirty.

The same but different and he found the difference
A surgeon's knife without an anaesthetic;
He had known of course that this happens
But had not guessed the pain of it or the panic,

And could not say 'My love', could hardly
Say anything at all, no longer knowing
Whom he was talking to but watched the water
Massing for action on the cold horizon.

LOUIS MACNEICE

298 EROS TURANNOS

She fears him, and will always ask
    What fated her to choose him,
She meets in his engaging mask
    All reasons to refuse him;
But what she meets and what she fears
Are less than are the downward years,
Drawn slowly to the foamless weirs
    Of age, were she to lose him.

Between a blurred sagacity
    That once had power to sound him,
And Love, that will not let him be
    The Judas that she found him,
Her pride assuages her almost,
As if it were alone the cost.—
He sees that he will not be lost,
    And waits and looks around him.

A sense of ocean and old trees
    Envelops and allures him;
Tradition, touching all he sees,
    Beguiles and reassures him;
And all her doubts of what he says
Are dimmed with what she knows of days—
Till even prejudice delays
    And fades, and she secures him.

The falling leaf inaugurates
    The reign of her confusion;
The pounding wave reverberates
    The dirge of her illusion;
And home, where passion lived and died,
Becomes a place where she can hide,
While all the town and harbor side
    Vibrate with her seclusion.

We tell you, tapping on our brows,
    The story as it should be,—
As if the story of a house
    Were told, or ever could be;
We'll have no kindly veil between
Her visions and those we have seen,—
As if we guessed what hers have been,
    Or what they are or would be.

Meanwhile we do no harm; for they
    That with a god have striven,
Not hearing much of what we say,
    Take what the god has given;
Though like waves breaking it may be,
Or like a changed familiar tree,
Or like a stairway to the sea
    Where down the blind are driven.

EDWIN ARLINGTON ROBINSON

299

It is the season of the sweet wild rose,
My Lady's emblem in the heart of me!
So golden-crownëd shines she gloriously,
And with that softest dream of blood she glows:
Mild as an evening heaven round Hesper bright!
I pluck the flower, and smell it, and revive
The time when in her eyes I stood alive.
I seem to look upon it out of Night.
Here's Madam, stepping hastily. Her whims
Bid her demand the flower, which I let drop.
As I proceed, I feel her sharply stop,
And crush it under heel with trembling limbs.
She joins me in a cat-like way, and talks
Of company, and even condescends
To utter laughing scandal of old friends.
These are the summer days, and these our walks.

GEORGE MEREDITH

300 SONG

When thou, poor excommunicate
　　From all the joys of love, shalt see
The full reward and glorious fate
　　Which my strong faith shall purchase me,
　　Then curse thine own inconstancy.

A fairer hand than thine shall cure
　　That heart, which thy false oaths did wound;
And to my soul a soul more pure
　　Than thine shall by Love's hand be bound,
　　And both with equal glory crown'd.

Then shalt thou weep, entreat, complain
　　To Love, as I did once to thee;
When all thy tears shall be as vain
　　As mine were then, for thou shalt be
　　Damn'd for thy false apostacy.

THOMAS CAREW

301 THE SCRUTINY

I

Why should you swear I am forsworn,
　　　Since thine I vow'd to be?
Lady, it is already morn,
　　　And 'twas last night I swore to thee
That fond impossibility.

ABSENCES, DOUBTS, DIVISION ✤ 273

II

Have I not lov'd thee much and long,
  A tedious twelve hours' space?
I must all other beauties wrong,
   And rob thee of a new embrace,
Could I still dote upon thy face.

III

Not, but all joy in thy brown hair
  By others may be found;
But I must search the black and fair
  Like skilful mineralists that sound
For treasure in unploughed-up ground.

IV

Then, if when I have lov'd my round,
  Thou prov'st the pleasant she,
With spoils of meaner beauties crown'd
  I laden will return to thee,
Ev'n sated with variety.

RICHARD LOVELACE

302 INCONSTANCY REPROVED

I do confess thou'rt smooth and fair,
 And I might have gone near to love thee,
Had I not found the slightest prayer
 That lips could move, had power to move thee;
But I can let thee now alone
As worthy to be loved by none.

I do confess thou'rt sweet; yet find
   Thee such an unthrift of thy sweets,
Thy favours are but like the wind
   That kisseth everything it meets:
And since thou canst with more than one,
Thou'rt worthy to be kissed by none.

The morning rose that untouched stands
   Armed with her briers, how sweet she smells!
But plucked and strained through ruder hands,
   Her sweets no longer with her dwells:
But scent and beauty both are gone,
And leaves fall from her, one by one.

Such fate ere long will thee betide
   When thou hast handled been awhile,
With sere flowers to be thrown aside;
   And I shall sigh, while some will smile,
To see thy love to every one
Hath brought thee to be loved by none.

SIR ROBERT AYTON

303   AGAINST CONSTANCY

Tell me no more of constancy,
   The frivolous pretence
Of cold age, narrow jealousy,
   Disease, and want of sense.

Let duller fools, on whom kind chance
   Some easy heart has thrown,
Despairing higher to advance,
   Be kind to one alone.

Old men and weak, whose idle flame
   Their own defects discovers,
Since changing can but spread their shame,
   Ought to be constant lovers.

But we, whose hearts do justly swell
   With no vainglorious pride,
Who know how we in love excel,
   Long to be often tried.

Then bring my bath, and strew my bed,
   As each kind night returns;
I'll change a mistress till I'me dead—
   And fate change me to worms.

JOHN WILMOT, EARL OF ROCHESTER

304   LOVE AND LIFE

All my past life is mine no more;
   The flying hours are gone,
Like transitory dreams given o'er
Whose images are kept in store
   By memory alone.

Whatever is to come is not:
   How can it then be mine?
The present moment's all my lot,
And that, as fast as it is got,
   Phyllis, is wholly thine.

Then talk not of inconstancy,
   False hearts, and broken vows;

If I, by miracle, can be
This livelong minute true to thee,
   'Tis all that heaven allows.

JOHN WILMOT, EARL OF ROCHESTER

305   THE FOREBODING

Looking by chance in at the open window
   I saw my own self seated in his chair
With gaze abstracted, furrowed forehead,
   Unkempt hair.

I thought that I had suddenly come to die,
   That to a cold corpse this was my farewell,
Until the pen moved slowly upon paper
   And tears fell.

He had written a name, yours, in printed letters:
   One word on which bemusedly to pore—
No protest, no desire, your naked name,
   Nothing more.

Would it be tomorrow, would it be next year?
   But the vision was not false, this much I knew;
And I turned angrily from the open window
   Aghast at you.

Why never a warning, either by speech or look,
   That the love you cruelly gave me could not last?
Already it was too late: the bait swallowed,
   The hook fast.

ROBERT GRAVES

306

Ask me no more: the moon may draw the sea;
   The cloud may stoop from heaven and take the shape
   With fold to fold, of mountain or of cape;
But O too fond, when have I answer'd thee?
                    Ask me no more.

Ask me no more: what answer should I give?
   I love not hollow cheek or faded eye:
   Yet, O my friend, I will not have thee die!
Ask me no more, lest I should bid thee live;
                    Ask me no more.

Ask me no more: thy fate and mine are seal'd,
   I strove against the stream and all in vain;
   Let the great river take me to the main:
No more, dear love, for at a touch I yield;
                    Ask me no more.

ALFRED TENNYSON

307

Love is a law, a discord of such force
That 'twixt our sense and reason makes divorce.
Love's a desire that to obtain betime
We lose an age of years pluck'd from our prime,
Love is a thing to which we soon consent,
As soon refuse, but sooner far repent.
Then what must women be that are the cause,
That Love hath life? that Lovers feel such laws?
They're like the winds upon Lapanthae's shores,

That still are changing. Oh then love no more.
A woman's love is like that Syrian flow'r
That buds, and spreads, and withers in an hour.

ANON.

308

Oh no more, no more, too late
Sighs are spent; the burning tapers
Of a life as chaste as Fate,
Pure as are unwritten papers,
   Are burnt out: no heat, no light
   Now remains, 'tis ever night.
Love is dead, let lovers' eyes,
   Lock'd in endless dreams,
   Th'extreme of all extremes,
Ope no more, for now Love dies,
   Now Love dies, implying
Love's martyrs must be ever, ever dying.

JOHN FORD

309 ANNIHILATION

While the blue noon above us arches
And the poplar sheds disconsolate leaves,
Tell me again why love bewitches
And what love gives.

Is it the trembling finger that traces
The eyebrow's curve, the curve of the cheek?
The mouth that quivers, while the hand caresses,
But cannot speak?

No, not these, not in these is hidden
The secret, more than in other things:
Not only the touch of a hand can gladden
Till the blood sings.

It is the leaf which falls between us,
The bell that murmurs, the shadows that move,
The autumnal sunlight that fades upon us,
These things are love.

It is the 'No, let us sit here longer,'
The 'Wait till to-morrow,' the 'Once I knew'—
These trifles, said as you touch my finger
And the clock strikes two.

The world is intricate, and we are nothing.
It is the complex world of grass,
The twig on the path, a look of loathing,
Feelings that pass—

These are the secret; and I could hate you
When, as I lean for another kiss,
I see in your eyes that I do not meet you,
And that love is this.

Rock meeting rock can know love better
Than eyes that stare or lips that touch.
All that we know in love is bitter,
And it is not much.

CONRAD AIKEN

There was never nothing more me pained,
Nor nothing more me moved,
As when my sweet heart her complained
That ever she me loved.
   Alas the while!

With piteous look she said and sighed:
Alas, what aileth me
To love and set my wealth so light
On him that loveth not me?
   Alas the while!

Was I not well void of all pain,
When that nothing me grieved?
And now with sorrows I must complain,
And cannot be relieved.
   Alas the while!

My restful nights and joyful days
Since I began to love
Be take from me; all thing decays,
Yet can I not remove.
   Alas the while!

She wept and wrung her hands withal,
The tears fell in my neck;
She turned her face and let it fall;
Scarcely therewith could speak.
   Alas the while!

Her pains tormented me so sore
That comfort had I none,
But cursed my fortune more and more
To see her sob and groan:
   Alas the while!

SIR THOMAS WYATT

311 ESTHÉTIQUE

La Femme mûr ou jeune fille,
J'en ai frôlé toutes les sortes,
Des faciles, des difficiles.
Voici, l'avis que j'en rapporte:

C'est des fleurs diversement mises,
Aux airs fiers ou seuls selon l'heure,
Nul cri sur elles n'a de prise;
Nous jouissons, Elle demeure.

Rien ne les tient, rien ne les fâche,
Elles veulent qu'on les trouve belles,
Qu'on le leur râle et leur rabâche,
Et qu'on les use comme telles;

Sans souci de serments, de bagues,
Suçons le peu qu'elles nous donnent,
Notre respect peut être vague,
Leurs yeux sont hauts et monotones.

Cueillons sans espoirs et sans drames,
La chair vieillit après les roses;
Oh! parcourons le plus de gammes!
Car il n'y a pas autre chose.

JULES LAFORGUE

312 UPON HIS LEAVING HIS MISTRESS

'Tis not that I am weary grown
Of being yours, and yours alone;
But with what face can I incline
To damn you to be only mine?

You, whom some kinder power did fashion,
By merit and by inclination,
The joy at least of one whole nation.

Let meaner spirits of your sex
With humbler aims their thoughts perplex,
And boast if by their arts they can
Contrive to make *one* happy man;
  Whilst, moved by an impartial sense,
  Favours like nature you dispense
  With universal influence.

See, the kind seed-receiving earth
To every grain affords a birth.
On her no showers unwelcome fall;
Her willing womb retains 'em all.
  And shall my Celia be confined?
  No! Live up to thy mighty mind,
  And be the mistress of mankind.

JOHN WILMOT, EARL OF ROCHESTER

313 AN APPEAL TO CATS IN THE BUSINESS OF LOVE

Ye cats that at midnight spit love at each other,
Who best feel the pangs of a passionate lover,
I appeal to your scratches and your tattered fur,
If the business of love be no more than to purr.
Old Lady Grimalkin with her gooseberry eyes
Knew some thing when a kitten, for why she was wise;
You find by experience, the love-fit's soon o'er,
Puss! Puss! lasts not long, but turns to *Cat-whore!*

Men ride many miles,
Cats tread many tiles,
Both hazard their necks in the fray;
Only cats, when they fall
From a house or a wall,
Keep their feet, mount their tails, and away!

THOMAS FLATMAN

314 THE APPARITION

When by thy scorn, O murd'ress, I am dead,
　And that thou thinkst thee free
From all solicitation from me,
Then shall my ghost come to thy bed,
And thee, fain'd vestal, in worse arms shall see;
Then thy sick taper will begin to wink,
And he, whose thou art then, being tir'd before,
Will, if thou stir, or pinch to wake him, think
　Thou call'st for more,
And in false sleep will from thee shrink,
And then poor aspen wretch, neglected thou
Bath'd in a cold quicksilver sweat wilt lie
A verier ghost than I;
What I will say, I will not tell thee now,
Lest that preserve thee; and since my love is spent,
I had rather thou shouldst painfully repent,
Than by my threat'nings rest still innocent.

JOHN DONNE

315 END OF THE AFFAIR

SHE I send my poisoned candies through the mail.
HE I set my bomb in your suburban road.
SHE I use this poisoned ink to make you die.
HE I haunt your marriage like the magic toad.
SHE My needling nib reddens your reptile eye.
HE It may. But I'm the black-legged spider now
    Upon your bedroom wall.
    Wait on his bed and watch me
    Till I fall.

GEOFFREY GRIGSON

316

Since there's no help, come let us kiss and part,
Nay, I have done: you get no more of me,
And I am glad, yea, glad with all my heart,
That thus so cleanly I myself can free,
Shake hands for ever, cancel all our vows,
And when we meet at any time again,
Be it not seen in either of our brows,
That we one jot of former love retain;
Now at the last gasp, of love's latest breath,
When, his pulse failing, passion speechless lies,
When faith is kneeling by his bed of death,
And innocence is closing up his eyes,
    Now if thou would'st, when all have given him over,
    From death to life, thou might'st him yet recover.

MICHAEL DRAYTON

317

Silent, you say, I'm grown of late,
Nor yield, as you do, to our fate?
Ah! that alone is truly pain
Of which we never can complain.

WALTER SAVAGE LANDOR

318

No, thou hast never griev'd but I griev'd too;
Smiled thou hast often when no smile of mine
Could answer it. The sun himself can give
But little colour to the desert sands.

WALTER SAVAGE LANDOR

319   THE SAD SONG

Away delights, go seek some other dwelling,
      For I must die:
Farewell, false Love, thy tongue is ever telling
      Lie after lie.
For ever let me rest now from thy smarts,
      Alas, for pity go,
      And fire their hearts
That have been hard to thee, mine was not so.

Never again deluding love shall know me,
      For I will die;
And all those griefs that think to over-grow me,
      Shall be as I:

For ever will I sleep, while poor maids cry,
        Alas, for pity stay,
        And let us die
With thee, men cannot mock us in the clay.

JOHN FLETCHER

320 LAMENT OF THE MASTER OF ERSKINE

Depairt, depairt, depairt,
Alas! I must depairt
From her that has my hairt,
    With hairt full sore,
Aganis my will indeed,
And can find no remeid:
I wait the pains of deid
    Can do no more.

Now must I go, alas!
From sicht of her sweet face,
The ground of all my grace,
    And sovereign;
What chance that may fall me,
Sall I never merry be,
Unto the time I see
    My sweet again.

I go, and wat not where,
I wander here and there,
I weep and sichis sair
    With painis smart;

Now must I pass away, away,
In wilderness and wilsome way,
Alas! this woeful day
    We suld depairt!

My spreit does quake for dread,
My thirlit hairt does bleed,
My painis does exceed—
    What suld I say?
I, woeful wicht, alone,
Makand ane piteous moan,
Alas! my hairt is gone
    For ever and aye.

Through languor of my sweet
So thirlit is my spreit,
My days are most complete
    Through her absence:
Christ sen sho knew my smart,
Ingravit in my hairt,
Because I must depairt,
    From her presence.

Adieu, my awin sweet thing,
My joy and comforting,
My mirth and solacing
    Of erdly gloir:
Fair weel, my lady bricht,
And my remembrance richt;
Fare weel and have gude nicht:
    I say no more.

ALEXANDER SCOTT

The mill-stream, now that noises cease,
Is all that does not hold its peace;
Under the bridge it murmurs by,
And here are night and hell and I.

Who made the world I cannot tell;
'Tis made, and here am I in hell.
My hand, though now my knuckles bleed,
I never soiled with such a deed.

And so, no doubt, in time gone by,
Some have suffered more than I,
Who only spend the night alone
And strike my fist upon the stone.

A. E. HOUSMAN

322 WITHOUT HER

What of her glass without her? The blank grey
   There where the pool is blind of the moon's face.
   Her dress without her? The tossed empty space
Of cloud-rack whence the moon has passed away.
Her paths without her? Day's appointed sway
   Usurped by desolate night. Her pillowed place
   Without her? Tears, ah me! for love's good grace,
And cold forgetfulness of night or day.

What of the heart without her? Nay, poor heart,
   Of thee what word remains ere speech be still?
   A wayfarer by barren ways and chill,

Steep ways and weary, without her thou art,
Where the long cloud, the long wood's counterpart,
    Sheds doubled darkness up the labouring hill.

D. G. ROSSETTI

323

My life closed twice before its close—
It yet remains to see
If Immortality unveil
A third event to me

So huge, so hopeless to conceive
As these that twice befell.
Parting is all we know of heaven,
And all we need of hell.

EMILY DICKINSON

324 TO MARY: I SLEEP WITH THEE, AND WAKE WITH THEE

I sleep with thee, and wake with thee,
    And yet thou art not there;
I fill my arms with thoughts of thee,
    And press the common air.
Thy eyes are gazing upon mine,
    When thou art out of sight;
My lips are always touching thine,
    At morning, noon, and night.

I think and speak of other things
    To keep my mind at rest:
But still to thee my memory clings
    Like love in woman's breast.
I hide it from the world's wide eye,
    And think and speak contrary;
But soft the wind comes from the sky,
    And whispers tales of Mary.

The night wind whispers in my ear,
    The moon shines in my face;
A burden still of chilling fear
    I find in every place.
The breeze is whispering in the bush,
    And the dews fall from the tree,
All sighing on, and will not hush,
    Some pleasant tales of thee.

                                    JOHN CLARE

325 TO MARY: IT IS THE EVENING HOUR

It is the evening hour,
    How silent all doth lie,
The hornèd moon he shews his face
    In the river with the sky.
Just by the path on which we pass,
The flaggy lake lies still as glass.

Spirit of her I love,
    Whispering to me,
Stories of sweet visions, as I rove,
Here stop, and crop with me
Sweet flowers that in the still hour grew,
We'll take them home, nor shake off the bright dew.

Mary, or sweet spirit of thee,
    As the bright sun shines to-morrow,
Thy dark eyes these flowers shall see,
    Gathered by me in sorrow,
In the still hour when my mind was free
To walk alone—yet wish I walk'd with thee.

JOHN CLARE

326

Over! the sweet summer closes,
    The reign of the roses is done;
Over and gone with the roses,
    And over and gone with the sun.

Over! the sweet summer closes,
    And never a flower at the close;
Over and gone with the roses,
    And winter again and the snows.

ALFRED TENNYSON

327

Oft have I mused, but now at length I find,
    Why those that die, men say they do depart:
Depart, a word so gentle to my mind,
    Weakly did seem to paint death's ugly dart.

But now the stars with their strange course do bind
    Me one to leave, with whom I leave my heart.
I hear a cry of spirits faint and blind,
    That parting thus my chiefest part I part.

Part of my life, the loathed part to me,
　Lives to impart my weary clay some breath.
But that good part, wherein all comforts be,
　Now dead, doth shew departure is a death.
　　Yea worse than death, death parts both woe and joy,
　　From joy I part still living in annoy.

SIR PHILIP SIDNEY

328　TWO SONNETS FROM MONNA INNOMINATA

i

'Era già l'ora che volge il desio.' DANTE.
'Ricorro al tempo ch' io vi vidi prima.' PETRARCA.

I wish I could remember that first day,
　First hour, first moment of your meeting me,
　If bright or dim the season, it might be
Summer or Winter for aught I can say;
So unrecorded did it slip away,
　So blind was I to see and to foresee,
　So dull to mark the budding of my tree
That would not blossom yet for many a May.
If only I could recollect it, such
　A day of days! I let it come and go
　As traceless as a thaw of bygone snow;
It seemed to mean so little, meant so much;
If only now I could recall that touch,
　First touch of hand in hand—Did one but know!

ii

'E la Sua Volontade e nostra pace.' DANTE.
'Sol con questi pensier, con altre chiome.' PETRARCA.

Youth gone, and beauty gone if ever there
  Dwelt beauty in so poor a face as this;
    Youth gone and beauty, what remains of bliss?
I will not bind fresh roses in my hair,
To shame a cheek at best but little fair,—
  Leave youth his roses, who can bear a thorn,—
I will not seek for blossoms anywhere,
  Except such common flowers as blow with corn.
Youth gone and beauty gone, what doth remain?
  The longing of a heart pent up forlorn,
    A silent heart whose silence loves and longs;
    The silence of a heart which sang its songs
  While youth and beauty made a summer morn,
Silence of love that cannot sing again.

CHRISTINA ROSSETTI

329

Have I, this moment, led thee from the beach
Into the boat? now far beyond my reach!
Stand there a little while, and wave once more
That 'kerchief; but may none upon the shore
Dare think the fond salute was meant for him!
Dizzily on the plashing water swim
My heavy eyes, and sometimes can attain
Thy lovely form, which tears bear off again.
In vain have they now ceast; it now is gone
Too far for sight, and leaves me here alone.

O could I hear the creaking of the mast!
I curse it present, I regret it past.

WALTER SAVAGE LANDOR

330

O fond, but fickle and untrue,
Ianthe take my last adieu.
Your heart one day will ask you why
You forced from me this farewell sigh.
Have you not feign'd that friends reprove
The mask of Friendship worn by Love?
Feign'd, that they whisper'd you should be
The same to others as to me?
Ah! little knew they what they said!
How would they blush to be obey'd!
   Too swiftly roll'd the wheels when last
These woods and airy downs we past.
Fain would we trace the winding path,
And hardly wisht for blissful Bath.
At every spring you caught my arm,
And every pebble roll'd alarm.
On me was turn'd that face divine,
The view was on the right so fine:
I smiled . . those conscious eyes withdrew . .
The left was now the finer view.
Each trembled for detected wiles,
And blushes tinged our fading smiles.
But Love turns Terror into jest . .
We laught, we kist, and we confest.
Laugh, kisses, confidence are past,
And Love goes too . . but goes the last.

WALTER SAVAGE LANDOR

If we shall live, we live:
  If we shall die, we die:
If we live we shall meet again:
    But to-night, good-bye.
One word, let but one be heard—
    What, not one word?

If we sleep we shall wake again
    And see to-morrow's light:
If we wake, we shall meet again:
    But to-night, good-night.
    Good-night, my lost and found—
      Still not a sound?

    If we live, we must part:
If we die, we part in pain:
    If we die, we shall part
    Only to meet again.
By those tears on either cheek,
    To-morrow you will speak.

    To meet, worth living for:
    Worth dying for, to meet.
    To meet, worth parting for:
    Bitter forgot in sweet.
    To meet, worth parting before,
    Never to part more.

11 *June* 1864.

CHRISTINA ROSSETTI

Take this kiss upon the brow!
And, in parting from you now,
Thus much let me avow—
You are not wrong, who deem
That my days have been a dream:
Yet if hope has flown away
In a night, or in a day,
In a vision, or in none,
Is it therefore the less *gone*?
All that we see or seem
Is but a dream within a dream.

I stand amid the roar
Of a surf-tormented shore,
And I hold within my hand
Grains of the golden sand—
How few! yet how they creep
Through my fingers to the deep,
While I weep—while I weep!
O God! can I not grasp
Them with a tighter clasp?
O God! can I not save
One from the pitiless wave?
Is *all* that we see or seem
But a dream within a dream?

EDGAR ALLAN POE

333 LA FIGLIA CHE PIANGE

O QUAM TE MEMOREM VIRGO . . .

Stand on the highest pavement of the stair—
Lean on a garden urn—
Weave, weave the sunlight in your hair—
Clasp your flowers to you with a pained surprise—
Fling them to the ground and turn
With a fugitive resentment in your eyes:
But weave, weave the sunlight in your hair.

So I would have had him leave,
So I would have had her stand and grieve,
So he would have left
As the soul leaves the body torn and bruised,
As the mind deserts the body it has used.
I should find
Some way incomparably light and deft,
Some way we both should understand,
Simple and faithless as a smile and shake of the hand.

She turned away, but with the autumn weather
Compelled my imagination many days,
Many days and many hours:
Her hair over her arms and her arms full of flowers.
And I wonder how they should have been together!
I should have lost a gesture and a pose.
Sometimes these cogitations still amaze
The troubled midnight and the noon's repose.

T. S. ELIOT

334

Quondam was I in my lady's grace,
I think as well as now be you;
And when that you have trad the trace,
Then shall you know my words be true,
    That quondam was I.

Quondam was I. She said for ever:
That lasted but a short while;
Promise made not to dissever.
I thought she laugh'd—she did but smile,
    Then quondam was I.

Quondam was I: he that full oft lay
In her arms with kisses many one.
It is enough that this I may say,
Though among the moo now I be gone,
    Yet quondam was I.

Quondam was I. Yet she will you tell
That since the hour she was first born
She never loved none half so well
As you. But what altho she had sworn,
    Sure quondam was I.

SIR THOMAS WYATT

335 MAY

I cannot tell you how it was;
But this I know: it came to pass—
Upon a bright and breezy day
When May was young, ah pleasant May!

As yet the poppies were not born
Between the blades of tender corn;
The last eggs had not hatched as yet,
Nor any bird forgone its mate.

I cannot tell you what it was;
But this I know: it did but pass.
It passed away with sunny May,
With all sweet things it passed away,
And left me old, and cold, and grey.

20 November 1855.

CHRISTINA ROSSETTI

336 TWICE

I took my heart in my hand,
  (O my love, O my love),
I said: Let me fall or stand,
  Let me live or die,
But this once hear me speak—
  (O my love, O my love)—
Yet a woman's words are weak;
  You should speak, not I.

You took my heart in your hand
  With a friendly smile,
With a critical eye you scanned,
  Then set it down,
And said: It is still unripe,
  Better wait awhile;
Wait while the skylarks pipe,
  Till the corn grows brown.

As you set it down it broke—
  Broke, but I did not wince;

I smiled at the speech you spoke,
　　At your judgment that I heard:
But I have not often smiled
　　Since then, nor questioned since,
Nor cared for corn-flowers wild,
　　Nor sung with the singing bird.

I take my heart in my hand,
　　O my God, O my God,
My broken heart in my hand:
　　Thou hast seen, judge Thou.
My hope was written on sand,
　　O my God, O my God:
Now let Thy judgment stand—
　　Yea, judge me now.

This contemned of a man,
　　This marred one heedless day,
This heart take Thou to scan
　　Both within and without:
Refine with fire its gold,
　　Purge Thou its dross away—
Yea, hold it in Thy hold,
　　Whence none can pluck it out.

I take my heart in my hand—
　　I shall not die, but live—
Before Thy face I stand;
　　I, for Thou callest such:
All that I have I bring,
　　All that I am I give;
Smile Thou and I shall sing,
　　But shall not question much.

June 1864.

CHRISTINA ROSSETTI

337

I loved a child of this countrie,
And so I wend he had do me;
Now my-self the sooth I see,
That he is far.

> *Were it undo that is y-do*
> *I would be-war.*

He said to me he would be true,
And change me for none other new;
Now I sykke and am pale of hue,
For he is far.

> *Were it undo that is y-do*
> *I would be-war.*

He said his saws he would fulfil,
Therefore I let him have all his will;
Now I sykke and mourne still,
For he is far.

> *Were it undo that is y-do*
> *I would be-war.*

ANON.

338 GRIEF OF A GIRL'S HEART

(FROM THE IRISH)

O Donal Oge, if you go across the sea,
Bring myself with you and do not forget it;
And you will have a sweetheart for fair days and market days,
And the daughter of the King of Greece beside you at night.

It is late last night the dog was speaking of you;
The snipe was speaking of you in her deep marsh.
It is you are the lonely bird through the woods;
And that you may be without a mate until you find me.

You promised me, and you said a lie to me,
That you would be before me where the sheep are flocked;
I gave a whistle and three hundred cries to you,
And I found nothing there but a bleating lamb.

You promised me a thing that was hard for you,
A ship of gold under a silver mast;
Twelve towns with a market in all of them,
And a fine white court by the side of the sea.

You promised me a thing that is not possible,
That you would give me gloves of the skin of a fish;
That you would give me shoes of the skin of a bird;
And a suit of the dearest silk in Ireland.

O Donal Oge, it is I would be better to you
Than a high, proud, spendthrift lady:
I would milk the cow; I would bring help to you;
And if you were hard pressed, I would strike a blow for you.

O, ochone, and it's not with hunger
Or with wanting food, or drink, or sleep,
That I am growing thin, and my life is shortened;
But it is the love of a young man has withered me away.

It is early in the morning that I saw him coming,
Going along the road on the back of a horse;
He did not come to me; he made nothing of me;
And it is on my way home that I cried my fill.

When I go by myself to the Well of Loneliness,
I sit down and I go through my trouble;
When I see the world and do not see my boy,
He that has an amber shade in his hair.

It was on that Sunday I gave my love to you;
The Sunday that is last before Easter Sunday.
And myself on my knees reading the Passion;
And my two eyes giving love to you for ever.

O, aya! my mother, give myself to him;
And give him all that you have in the world;
Get out yourself to ask for alms,
And do not come back and forward looking for me.

My mother said to me not to be talking with you, to-day,
Or to-morrow, or on Sunday;
It was a bad time she took for telling me that;
It was shutting the door after the house was robbed.

My heart is as black as the blackness of the sloe,
Or as the black coal that is on the smith's forge;
Or as the sole of a shoe left in white halls;
It was you put that darkness over my life.

You have taken the east from me; you have taken the west from me,
You have taken what is before me and what is behind me;
You have taken the moon, you have taken the sun from me,
And my fear is great that you have taken God from me!

AUGUSTA GREGORY

Vous aviez mon cœur,
Moi, j'avais le vôtre:
Un cœur pour un cœur;
Bonheur pour bonheure!

Le vôtre est rendu;
Je n'en ai plus d'autre,
Le vôtre est rendu,
Le mien est perdu.

La feuille et la fleur
Et le fruit lui-même,
La feuille et la fleur,
L'encens, la couleur:

Qu'en avez-vous fait,
Mon maître suprême?
Qu'en avez-vous fait,
De ce doux bienfait?

Comme un pauvre enfant,
Quitté par sa mère,
Comme un pauvre enfant,
Que rien ne défend:

Vous me laissez là,
Dans ma vie amère;
Vous me laissez là,
Et Dieu voit cela!

Savez-vous qu'un jour,
L'homme est seul au monde?
Savez-vous qu'un jour,
Il revolt l'amour?

Vous appellerez,
Sans qu'on vous réponde,
Vous appellerez;
Et vous songerez! . . .

Vous viendrez rêvant.
Sonner à ma porte;
Ami comme avant,
Vous viendrez rêvant.

Et l'on vous dira:
'Personne . . . elle est morte.'
On vous le dira:
Mais, qui vous plaindra!

MARCELINE DESBORDES-VALMORE

340

Farewell, all my welfare,
My shoe is trod awry;
Now I may cark and care
To sing *lullay by by*.
Alas, what shall I do thereto?
There is no shift to help me now.

Who made it such offence
To love for love again?
God wot that my pretence
Was but to ease his pain;
For I had ruth to see his woe.
Alas, more fool, why did I so?

For he from me is gone
And makes thereat a game,
And hath left me alone
To suffer sorrow and shame.
Alas, he is unkind doubtless
To leave me thus all comfortless.

It is a grievous smart
To suffer pains and sorrow;
But most it grieved my heart
He laid his faith to borrow:
And falsehood hath his faith and truth,
And he forsworn by many an oath.

All ye lovers, perdy,
Have cause to blame his deed,
Which shall example be
To let you off your speed;
Let never woman again
Trust to such words as men can fain.

For I, unto my cost,
Am warning to you all
That they whom you trust most
Soonest deceive you shall;
But, complaint cannot redress
Of my great grief the great excess.

SIR THOMAS WYATT

341 LA PROMENADE D'AUTOMNE

Te souvient-il, ô mon âme, ô ma vie,
D'un jour d'automne et pâle et languissant?
Il semblait dire un adieu gémissant
Aux bois qu'il attristait de sa mélancolie.

Les oiseaux dans les airs ne chantaient plus l'espoir;
Une froide rosée enveloppait leurs ailes,
Et, rappelant au nid leurs compagnes fidèles,
Sur des rameaux sans fleurs ils attendaient le soir.

Les troupeaux, à regret menés aux pâturages,
    N'y trouvaient plus que des herbes sauvages;
Et le pâtre, oubliant sa rustique chanson,
Partageait le silence et le deuil du vallon.
    Rien ne charmait l'ennui de la nature.
La feuille qui perdait sa riante couleur,
Les coteaux dépouillés de leur verte parure,
Tout demandait au ciel un rayon de chaleur.

Seule, je m'éloignais d'une fête bruyante;
Je fuyais tes regards, je cherchais ma raison:
Mais la langueur des champs, leur tristesse attrayante,
A ma langueur secrète ajoutaient leur poison.
Sans but et sans espoir suivant ma rêverie,
Je portais au hasard un pas timide et lent;
L'Amour m'enveloppa de ton ombre chérie,
Et, malgré la saison, l'air me parut brûlant.

Je voulais, mais en vain, par un effort suprême,
En me sauvant de toi, me sauver de moi-même;
Mon œil, voilé de pleurs, à la terre attaché,
Par un charme invincible en fut comme arraché.
A travers les brouillards, une image légère
Fit palpiter mon sein de tendresse et d'effroi;
Le soleil reparaît, l'environne, l'éclaire,
Il entr'ouvre les cieux. . . . Tu parus devant moi.
Je n'osai te parler: interdite, rêveuse,
Enchaînée et soumise à ce trouble enchanteur,
Je n'osai te parler: pourtant j'étais heureuse;
Je devinai ton âme, et j'entendis mon cœur.

Mais, quand ta main pressa ma main tremblante,
Quand un frisson léger fit tressaillir mon corps,
Quand mon front se couvrit d'un rougeur brûlante,
    Dieu! qu'est-ce donc que je sentis alors?
J'oubliai de te fuir, j'oubliai de te craindre;
Pour la première fois ta bouche osa se plaindre,
Ma douleur à la tienne osa se révéler,
Et mon âme vers toi fut près de s'exhaler.
    Il m'en souvient! T'en souvient-il, ma vie,
        De ce tourment délicieux,
De ces mots arrachés à ta mélancolie:
        «Ah! si je souffre, on souffre aux cieux! »

Des bois nul autre aveu ne troubla le silence.
Ce jour fut de nos jours le plus beau, le plus doux;
Prêt à s'éteindre, enfin il s'arrêta sur nous,
Et sa fuite à mon cœur présagea ton absence:
    L'âme du monde éclaira notre amour;
Je vis ses derniers feux mourir sous un nuage;
Et dans nos cœurs brisés, désunis sans retour,
    Il n'en reste plus que l'image!

MARCELINE DESBORDES-VALMORE

342

I do not look for love that is a dream—
    I only seek for courage to be still;
    To bear my grief with an unbending will,
And when I am a-weary not to seem.
Let the round world roll on; let the sun beam;
    Let the wind blow, and let the rivers fill
    The everlasting sea, and on the hill
The palms almost touch heaven, as children deem.

And, though young spring and summer pass away,
   And autumn and cold winter come again,
   And though my soul, being tired of its pain,
Pass from the ancient earth, and though my clay
   Return to dust, my tongue shall not complain;—
No man shall mock me after this my day.

   18 *February* 1848.

CHRISTINA ROSSETTI

343 SONG

She sat and sang alway
   By the green margin of a stream,
Watching the fishes leap and play
   Beneath the glad sunbeam.

I sat and wept alway
   Beneath the moon's most shadowy beam,
Watching the blossoms of the May
   Weep leaves into the stream.

I wept for memory;
   She sang for hope that is so fair:
My tears were swallowed by the sea;
   Her songs died on the air.

   26 *November* 1848.

CHRISTINA ROSSETTI

344 BITTER FOR SWEET

Summer is gone with all its roses.
   Its sun and perfumes and sweet flowers,
   Its warm air and refreshing showers:
      And even Autumn closes.

Yea, Autumn's chilly self is going,
   And Winter comes which is yet colder;
   Each day the hoar-frost waxes bolder,
      And the last buds cease blowing.

1 *December* 1848.

CHRISTINA ROSSETTI

345 SONG

When I am dead, my dearest,
   Sing no sad songs for me;
Plant thou no roses at my head,
   Nor shady cypress tree:
Be the green grass above me
   With showers and dewdrops wet:
And if thou wilt, remember,
   And if thou wilt, forget.

I shall not see the shadows,
   I shall not feel the rain:
I shall not hear the nightingale
   Sing on as if in pain:

And dreaming through the twilight
    That doth not rise nor set,
Haply I may remember,
    And haply may forget.

12 *December* 1848.

CHRISTINA ROSSETTI

346   LOVE AND AGE

Loves flies with bow unstrung when Time appears,
And trembles at the approach of heavy years.
A few bright feathers leaves he in his flight,
Quite beyond recall, but not forgotten quite.

WALTER SAVAGE LANDOR

347

The Loves who many years held all my mind,
A charge so troublesome at last resign'd.
Among my books a feather here and there
Tells what the inmates of my study were.
Strong for no wrestle, ready for no race,
They only serve to mark the left-off place.
'Twas theirs to dip in the tempestuous waves,
'Twas theirs to loiter in cool summer caves;
But in the desert where no herb is green
Not one, the latest of the flight, is seen.

WALTER SAVAGE LANDOR

348

That time of year thou mayst in me behold,
When yellow leaves, or none, or few do hang
Upon those boughs which shake against the cold,
Bare ruin'd choirs, where late the sweet birds sang.
In me thou see'st the twilight of such day,
As after sunset fadeth in the west,
Which by and by black night doth take away,
Death's second self that seals up all in rest.
In me thou see'st the glowing of such fire,
That on the ashes of his youth doth lie,
As the death bed, whereon it must expire,
Consum'd with that which it was nourish'd by.
  This thou perceiv'st, which makes thy love more strong,
  To love that well, which thou must leave ere long.

WILLIAM SHAKESPEARE

6

LOVE RENOUNCED AND LOVE IN DEATH

349

Underneath a cypress shade, the Queen of Love sat mourning,
Casting down the rosy wreaths her heavenly brow adorning:
Quenching fiery sighs with tears, but yet her heart still burning.

For within the shady bourne, the cause of her complaining,
Myrrha's son the leafy bowers did haunt, her love disdaining,
Counting all her true desires in his fond thoughts but feigning.

Why is youth with beauty graced, unfeeling judge of kindness,
Spotting love with the foul report of cruelty and blindness,
Forcing to unkind complaints the Queen of all divineness?

Stint thy tears, fair sea-born Queen, and grief in vain lamented,
When desire hath burnt his heart that thee hath discontented,
Then too late the scorn of youth by age shall be repented.

ANON.

350

Blow, blow, thou winter wind,
Thou art not so unkind, as man's ingratitude,
Thy tooth is not so keen, because thou art not seen,
    Although thy breath be rude.
Heigh ho, sing heigh ho, unto the green holly,
Most friendship, is feigning; most loving, mere folly:
    Then heigh ho, the holly,
    This life is most jolly.

Freeze, freeze, thou bitter sky that dost not bite so nigh
     As benefits forgot:
Though thou the waters warp, thy sting is not so sharp,
     As friend remembered not.
Heigh ho, sing heigh ho, unto the green holly,
Most friendship, is feigning; most loving, mere folly:
          Then heigh ho, the holly,
          This life is most jolly.

WILLIAM SHAKESPEARE

351 A RENOUNCING OF LOVE

Farewell, Love, and all thy laws for ever:
Thy baited hooks shall tangle me no more;
Senec and Plato call me from thy lore,
To perfect wealth my wit for to endeavour.
In blind error when I did persever,
Thy sharp repulse, that pricketh ay so sore,
Hath taught me to set in trifles no store,
And scape forth, since liberty is lever.
Therefore, farewell: go trouble younger hearts,
And in me claim no more authority;
With idle youth go use thy property,
And thereon spend thy many brittle darts;
For hitherto though I have lost all my time,
Me lusteth no longer rotten boughs to climb.

SIR THOMAS WYATT

Full many sing to me and thee
Their riches gather'd by the sea;
    But I will sing, for I'm footsore,
    The burthen of the barren shore.

The hue of love how lively shown
In this sole found cerulean stone
    By twenty leagues of ocean roar.
    O, burthen of the barren shore!

And these few crystal fragments bright,
As clear as truth, as strong as right,
    I found in footing twenty more.
    O, burthen of the barren shore!

And how far did I go for this
Small, precious piece of ambergris?
    Of weary leagues I went threescore.
    O, burthen of the barren shore!

The sand is poor, the sea is rich,
And I, I am I know not which;
    And well it were to know no more
    The burthen of the barren shore!

COVENTRY PATMORE

353

i

Out in the yellow meadows, where the bee
Hums by us with the honey of the Spring,
And showers of sweet notes from the larks on wing
Are dropping like a noon-dew, wander we.

Or is it now? or was it then? for now,
As then, the larks from running rings pour showers:
The golden foot of May is on the flowers,
And friendly shadows dance upon her brow.
What's this, when Nature swears there is no change
To challenge eyesight? Now, as then, the grace
Of heaven seems holding earth in its embrace.
Nor eyes, nor heart, has she to feel it strange?
Look, woman, in the West. There wilt thou see
An amber cradle near the sun's decline:
Within it, featured even in death divine,
Is lying a dead infant, slain by thee.

ii

Not solely that the Future she destroys,
And the fair life which in the distance lies
For all men, beckoning out from dim rich skies:
Nor that the passing hour's supporting joys
Have lost the keen-edged flavour, which begat
Distinction in old times, and still should breed
Sweet Memory, and Hope,—earth's modest seed,
And heaven's high-prompting: not that the world is flat
Since that soft-luring creature I embraced
Among the children of Illusion went:
Methinks with all this loss I were content,
If the mad Past, on which my foot is based,
Were firm, or might be blotted: but the whole
Of life is mixed: the mocking Past will stay:
And if I drink oblivion of a day,
So shorten I the stature of my soul.

GEORGE MEREDITH

354

Farewell sweet boy, complain not of my truth;
Thy mother lov'd thee not with more devotion;
For to thy boy's play I gave all my youth,
Young master, I did hope for your promotion.

While some sought honours, princes' thoughts observing,
Many woo'd Fame, the child of pain and anguish,
Others judg'd inward good a chief deserving,
I in thy wanton visions joy'd to languish.

I bow'd not to thy image for succession,
Nor bound thy bow to shoot reformed kindness,
Thy plays of hope and fear were my confession,
The spectacles to my life was thy blindness;
   But Cupid now farewell, I will go play me,
    With thoughts that please me less and less betray me.

FULKE GREVILLE, LORD BROOKE

355 WHEN YOU ARE OLD

When you are old and gray and full of sleep,
And nodding by the fire, take down this book,
And slowly read, and dream of the soft look
Your eyes had once, and of their shadows deep;

How many loved your moments of glad grace,
And loved your beauty with love false or true;
But one man loved the pilgrim soul in you,
And loved the sorrows of your changing face.

And bending down beside the glowing bars
Murmur, a little sadly, how love fled
And paced upon the mountains overhead
And hid his face amid a crowd of stars.

W. B. YEATS
(after the French of RONSARD[1])

356

Leave me, O Love, which reachest but to dust,
And thou my mind aspire to higher things:
Grow rich in that which never taketh rust:
Whatever fades, but fading pleasure brings.

Draw in thy beams, and humble all thy might,
To that sweet yoke, where lasting freedoms be:
Which breaks the clouds and opens forth the light,
That doth both shine and give us sight to see.

O take fast hold, let that light be thy guide,
In this small course which birth draws out to death,
And think how evil becometh him to slide,
Who seeketh heav'n, and comes of heav'nly breath.
  Then farewell, world, thy uttermost I see,
  Eternal Love, maintain thy life in me.

Splendidis longum valedico nugis.

SIR PHILIP SIDNEY

[1] p. 377.

357 I SAID TO LOVE

I said to Love,
'It is not now as in old days
When men adored thee and thy ways
        All else above;
Named thee the Boy, the Bright, the One
Who spread a heaven beneath the sun,'
        I said to Love.

I said to Love,
'We now know more of thee than then;
We were but weak in judgment when,
        With hearts abrim,
We clamoured thee that thou would'st please
Inflict on us thine agonies,'
        I said to him.

I said to him,
'Thou art not young, thou art not fair,
No elfin darts, no cherub air,
        Nor swan, nor dove
Are thine; but features pitiless,
And iron daggers of distress,'
        I said to Love.

'Depart then, Love! . . .
— Man's race shall perish, threatenest thou,
Without thy kindling coupling-vow?
The age to come the men of now
        Know nothing of—
We fear not such a threat from thee;
We are too old in apathy!
Mankind shall cease.—So let it be,'
        I said to Love.

THOMAS HARDY

358

Mark where the pressing wind shoots javelin-like
Its skeleton shadow on the broad-backed wave!
Here is a fitting spot to dig Love's grave;
Here where the ponderous breakers plunge and strike,
And dart their hissing tongues high up the sand:
In hearing of the ocean, and in sight
Of those ribbed wind-streaks running into white.
If I the death of Love had deeply planned,
I never could have made it half so sure,
As by the unblest kisses which upbraid
The full-waked sense; or failing that, degrade!
'Tis morning: but no morning can restore
What we have forfeited. I see no sin:
The wrong is mixed. In tragic life, God wot,
No villain need be! Passions spin the plot:
We are betrayed by what is false within.

GEORGE MEREDITH

359 UN VOYAGE À CYTHÈRE

Mon cœur, comme un oiseau, voltigeait tout joyeux
Et planait librement à l'entour des cordages;
Le navire roulait sous un ciel sans nuages,
Comme un ange enivré du soleil radieux.

Quelle est cette île triste et noire? — C'est Cythère,
Nous dit-on, un pays fameux dans les chansons,
Eldorado banal de tous les vieux garçons.
Regardez, après tout, c'est une pauvre terre.

—Ile des doux secrets et des fêtes du cœur!
De l'antique Vénus le superbe fantôme
Au-dessus de tes mers plane comme un arome,
Et charge les esprits d'amour et de langueur.

Belle île aux myrtes verts pleine de fleurs écloses,
Vénérée à jamais par toute nation.
Où les soupirs des cœurs en adoration
Roulent comme l'encens sur un jardin de roses

Ou le roucoulement éternel d'un ramier!
—Cythère n'était plus qu'un terrain des plus maigres,
Un désert rocailleux troublé par des cris aigres.
J'entrevoyais pourtant un objet singulier!

Ce n'était pas un temple aux ombres bocagères,
Où la jeune prêtresse, amoureuse des fleurs,
Allait, le corps brûlé de secrètes chaleurs,
Entre-bâillant sa robe aux brises passagères;

Mais voilà qu'en rasant la côte d'assez près
Pour troubler les oiseaux avec nos voiles blanches,
Nous vîmes que c'était un gibet à trois branches,
Du ciel se détachant en noir, comme un cyprès.

De féroces oiseaux perchés sur leur pâture
Détruisant avec rage un pendu déjà mûr,
Chacun plantant, comme un outil, son bec impur
Dans tous les coins saignants de cette pourriture;

Les yeux étaient deux trous, et du ventre effondré
Les intestins pesants lui coulaient sur les cuisses,
Et ses bourreaux gorgés de hideuses délices
L'avaient à coups de bec absolument châtré.

Sous les pieds, un troupeau de jaloux quadrupèdes,
Le museau relevé, tournoyait et rôdait;
Une plus grande bête au milieu s'agitait
Comme un exécuteur entouré de ses aides.

Habitant de Cythère, enfant d'un ciel si beau,
Silencieusement tu souffrais ces insultes
En expiation de tes infâmes cultes
Et des péchés qui t'ont interdit le tombeau.

Ridicule pendu, tes douleurs sont les miennes!
Je sentis à l'aspect de tes membres flottants,
Comme un vomissement, remonter vers mes dents
Le long fleuve de fiel des douleurs anciennes;

Devant toi, pauvre diable au souvenir si cher,
J'ai senti tous les becs et toutes les mâchoires
Des corbeaux lancinants et des panthères noires
Qui jadis aimaient tant à triturer ma chair.

—Le ciel était charmant, la mer était unie;
Pour moi tout était noir et sanglant désormais,
Hélas! et j'avais, comme en un suaire épais,
Le cœur enseveli dans cette allégorie.

Dans ton île, ô Vénus! je n'ai trouvé debout
Qu'un gibet symbolique où penchait mon image . . .
— Ah! Seigneur! donnez-moi la force et le courage
De contempler mon cœur et mon corps sans dégoût!

                                    CHARLES BAUDELAIRE

360 SONG

Love a woman? You're an ass!
　'Tis a most insipid passion
To choose out for your happiness
　The silliest part of God's creation.

Let the porter and the groom,
　Things designed for dirty slaves,
Drudge in fair Aurelia's womb
　To get supplies for age and graves.

Farewell, woman! I intend
　Henceforth every night to sit
With my lewd, well-natured friend,
　Drinking to engender wit.

Then give me health, wealth, mirth, and wine,
　And, if busy love entrenches,
There's a sweet, soft page of mine
　Does the trick worth forty wenches.

JOHN WILMOT, EARL OF ROCHESTER

361

i

Am I failing? For no longer can I cast
A glory round about this head of gold.
Glory she wears, but springing from the mould;
Not like the consecration of the Past!
Is my soul beggared? Something more than earth
I cry for still: I cannot be at peace
In having Love upon a mortal lease.
I cannot take the woman at her worth!

Where is the ancient wealth wherewith I clothed
Our human nakedness, and could endow
With spiritual splendour a white brow
That else had grinned at me the fact I loathed?
A kiss is but a kiss now! and no wave
Of a great flood that whirls me to the sea.
But, as you will! we'll sit contentedly,
And eat our pot of honey on the grave.

ii

What are we first? First, animals; and next
Intelligences at a leap; on whom
Pale lies the distant shadow of the tomb,
And all that draweth on the tomb for text.
Into which state comes Love, the crowning sun:
Beneath whose light the shadow loses form.
We are the lords of life, and life is warm.
Intelligence and instinct now are one.
But nature says: 'My children most they seem
When they least know me: therefore I decree
That they shall suffer.' Swift doth young Love flee,
And we stand wakened, shivering from our dream.
Then if we study Nature we are wise.
Thus do the few who live but with the day:
The scientific animals are they.—
Lady, this is my sonnet to your eyes.

GEORGE MEREDITH

362 THE COMET AT YELL'HAM

I

It bends far over Yell'ham Plain,
    And we, from Yell'ham Height,
Stand and regard its fiery train,
    So soon to swim from sight.

II

It will return long years hence, when
    As now its strange swift shine
Will fall on Yell'ham; but not then
    On that sweet form of thine.

THOMAS HARDY

363 LE PORTRAIT

La Maladie et la Mort font des cendres
De tout le feu qui pour nous flamboya.
De ces grands yeux si fervents et si tendres,
De cette bouche où mon cœur se noya,

De ces baisers puissants comme un dictame,
De ces transports plus vifs que des rayons,
Que reste-t-il? C'est affreux, ô mon âme!
Rien qu'un dessin fort pâle, aux trois crayons,

Qui, comme moi, meurt dans la solitude,
Et que le Temps, injurieux vieillard,
Chaque jour frotte avec son aile rude . . .

Noir assassin de la Vie et de l'Art,
Tu ne tueras jamais dans ma mémoire
Celle qui fut mon plaisir et ma gloire!

CHARLES BAUDELAIRE

364 THE AZALEA

There, where the sun shines first
Against our room,
She train'd the gold Azalea, whose perfume
She, Spring-like, from her breathing grace dispersed.
Last night the delicate crests of saffron bloom,
For this their dainty likeness watch'd and nurst,
Were just at point to burst.
At dawn I dream'd, O God, that she was dead,
And groan'd aloud upon my wretched bed,
And waked, ah, God, and did not waken her,
But lay, with eyes still closed,
Perfectly bless'd in the delicious sphere
By which I knew so well that she was near,
My heart to speechless thankfulness composed.
Till 'gan to stir
A dizzy somewhat in my troubled head—
It *was* the azalea's breath, and she *was* dead!
The warm night had the lingering buds disclosed,
And I had fall'n asleep with to my breast
A chance-found letter press'd
In which she said,
'So, till to-morrow eve, my Own, adieu!
Parting's well-paid with soon again to meet,
Soon in your arms to feel so small and sweet,
Sweet to myself that am so sweet to you!'

COVENTRY PATMORE

365 A DREAM OF DEATH

I dreamed that one had died in a strange place
Near no accustomed hand;
And they had nailed the boards above her face
The peasants of that land,
Wondering to lay her in that solitude,
And raised above her mound
A cross they had made out of two bits of wood,
And planted cypress round;
And left her to the indifferent stars above
Until I carved these words:
She was more beautiful than thy first love,
But now lies under boards.

W. B. YEATS

366 THE LEPER

Nothing is better, I well think,
    Than love; the hidden well-water
Is not so delicate to drink:
    This was well seen of me and her.

I served her in a royal house;
    I served her wine and curious meat.
For will to kiss between her brows
    I had no heart to sleep or eat.

Mere scorn God knows she had of me;
    A poor scribe, nowise great or fair,
Who plucked his clerk's hood back to see
    Her curled-up lips and amorous hair.

I vex my head with thinking this.
    Yea, though God always hated me,
And hates me now that I can kiss
    Her eyes, plait up her hair to see

How she then wore it on the brows,
    Yet am I glad to have her dead
Here in this wretched wattled house
    Where I can kiss her eyes and head.

Nothing is better, I well know,
    Than love; no amber in cold sea
Or gathered berries under snow:
    That is well seen of her and me.

Three thoughts I make my pleasure of:
    First I take heart and think of this:
That knight's gold hair she chose to love,
    His mouth she had such will to kiss.

Then I remember that sundawn
    I brought him by a privy way
Out at her lattice, and thereon
    What gracious words she found to say.

(Cold rushes for such little feet—
    Both feet could lie into my hand.
A marvel was it of my sweet
    Her upright body could so stand.)

'Sweet friend, God give you thank and grace;
    Now am I clean and whole of shame,
Nor shall men burn me in the face
    For my sweet fault that scandals them.'

I tell you over word by word.
    She, sitting edgewise on her bed,
Holding her feet, said thus. The third,
    A sweeter thing than these, I said.

God, that makes time and ruins it,
    And alters not, abiding God,
Changed with disease her body sweet,
    The body of love wherein she abode.

Love is more sweet and comelier
    Than a dove's throat strained out to sing.
All they spat out and cursed at her
    And cast her forth for a base thing.

They cursed her, seeing how God had wrought
    This curse to plague her, a curse of his.
Fools were they surely, seeing not
    How sweeter than all sweet she is.

He that had held her by the hair,
    With kissing lips blinding her eyes.
Felt her bright bosom, strained and bare,
    Sigh under him, with short mad cries

Out of her throat and sobbing mouth
    And body broken up with love,
With sweet hot tears his lips were loth
    Her own should taste the savour of,

Yea, he inside whose grasp all night
    Her fervent body leapt or lay,
Stained with sharp kisses red and white,
    Found her a plague to spurn away.

I hid her in this wattled house,
    I served her water and poor bread.
For joy to kiss between her brows
    Time upon time I was nigh dead.

Bread failed; we got but well-water
    And gathered grass with dropping seed.
I had such joy of kissing her,
    I had small care to sleep or feed.

Sometimes when service made me glad
    The sharp tears leapt between my lids,
Falling on her, such joy I had
    To do the service God forbids.

'I pray you let me be at peace,
    Get hence, make room for me to die.'
She said that: her poor lip would cease,
    Put up to mine, and turn to cry.

I said, 'Bethink yourself how love
    Fared in us twain, what either did;
Shall I unclothe my soul thereof?
    That I should do this, God forbid.'

Yea, though God hateth us, he knows
    That hardly in a little thing
Love faileth of the work it does
    Till it grow ripe for gathering.

Six months, and now my sweet is dead
    A trouble takes me; I know not
If all were done well, all well said,
    No word or tender deed forgot.

Too sweet, for the least part in her,
  To have shed life out by fragments; yet,
Could the close mouth catch breath and stir,
  I might see something I forget.

Six months, and I sit still and hold
  In two cold palms her cold two feet.
Her hair, half grey half ruined gold,
  Thrills me and burns me in kissing it.

Love bites and stings me through, to see
  Her keen face made of sunken bones.
Her worn-off eyelids madden me,
  That were shot through with purple once.

She said, 'Be good with me; I grow
  So tired for shame's sake, I shall die
If you say nothing:' even so.
  And she is dead now, and shame put by.

Yea, and the scorn she had of me
  In the old time, doubtless vexed her then.
I never should have kissed her. See
  What fools God's anger makes of men!

She might have loved me a little too,
  Had I been humbler for her sake.
But that new shame could make love new
  She saw not—yet her shame did make.

I took too much upon my love,
  Having for such mean service done
Her beauty and all the ways thereof,
  Her face and all the sweet thereon.

Yea, all this while I tended her,
  I know the old love held fast his part:
I know the old scorn waxed heavier,
  Mixed with sad wonder, in her heart.

It may be all my love went wrong—
  A scribe's work writ awry and blurred,
Scrawled after the blind evensong—
  Spoilt music with no perfect word.

But surely I would fain have done
  All things the best I could. Perchance
Because I failed, came short of one,
  She kept at heart that other man's.

I am grown blind with all these things:
  It may be now she hath in sight
Some better knowledge; still there clings
  The old question. Will not God do right?*

A. C. SWINBURNE

* En ce temps-là estoyt dans ce pays grand nombre de ladres et de meseaulx, ce dont le roy eut grand desplaisir, veu que Dieu dust en estre moult griefvement courroucé. Ores il advint qu'une noble damoyselle appelée Yolande de Sallières estant atteincte et touste guastée de ce vilain mal, tous ses amys et ses parens ayant devant leurs yeux la paour de Dieu la firent issir fors de leurs maisons et oncques ne voulurent recepvoir ni reconforter chose mauldicte de Dieu et à tous les hommes puante et abhominable. Ceste dame avoyt esté moult belle et gracieuse de formes, et de son corps elle estoyt large et de vie lascive. Pourtant nul des amans qui l'avoyent souventesfois accollée et baisée moult tendrement ne voulust plus héberger si laide femme et si détestable pescheresse. Ung seul clerc qui feut premièrement son lacquays et son entremetteur en matière d'amour la reçut chez luy et la récéla dans une petite cabane. Là mourut la meschinette de grande misère et de male mort: et après elle décéda ledist clerc qui pour grand amour l'avoyt six mois durant soignée, lavée, habillée et deshabillée tous les jours de ses mains propres. Mesme dist-on que ce meschant

homme et mauldict clerc se remémourant de la grande beauté passée
et guastée de ceste femme se délectoyt maintesfois à la baiser sur sa
bouche orde et lépreuse et l'accoller doulcement de ses mains amou-
reuses. Aussy est-il mort de ceste mesme maladie abhominable. Cecy
advint près Fontainebellant en Gastinois. Et quand ouyt le roy Philippe
ceste adventure moult en estoyt esmerveillé.

Grandes Chroniques de France, 1505.

367

One day I wrote her name upon the strand,
But came the waves and washed it away:
Again I wrote it with a second hand,
But came the tide, and made my pains his prey.
Vain man, said she, that dost in vain assay
A mortal thing so to immortalize,
For I myself shall like to this decay,
And eke my name be wiped out likewise.
Not so, (quod I) let baser things devise
To die in dust, but you shall live by fame:
My verse your virtues rare shall eternize,
And in the heavens write your glorious name:
Where, whenas Death shall all the world subdue,
Our love shall live, and later life renew.

EDMUND SPENSER

368

La blanche Aurore à peine finyssoit
D'orner son chef d'or luisant, et des roses,
Quand mon esprit, qui du tout perissoit
Au fons confus de tant diverses choses,
Revint à moy soubz les custodes closes

Pour plus me rendre envers Mort invincible.
     Mais toy qui as — toy seule — le possible
De donner heur à ma fatalité,
Tu me seras la myrrhe incorruptible
Contre les vers de ma mortalité.

MAURICE SCÈVE

369

How many paltry, foolish, painted things,
That now in coaches trouble ev'ry street,
Shall be forgotten, whom no poet sings,
Ere they be well wrapp'd in their winding-sheet?
Where I to thee eternity shall give,
When nothing else remaineth of these days,
And queens hereafter shall be glad to live
Upon the alms of thy superfluous praise;
Virgins and matrons reading these my rhymes,
Shall be so much delighted with thy story,
That they shall grieve they liv'd not in these times,
To have seen thee, their sex's only glory:
     So shalt thou fly above the vulgar throng,
     Still to survive in my immortal song.

MICHAEL DRAYTON

370

Si tu t' enquiers pourquoy sur mon tombeau
Lon auroit mys deux elementz contraires,
Comme tu voys estre le feu, et l'eau,
Entre elementz les deux plus adversaires:

J t' advertis, qu'ilz sont tresnecessaires
Pour te monstrer par signes evidentz,
Que si en moy ont esté residentz
Larmes et feu, bataille asprement rude:
Qu' apres ma mort encores cy dedens
Je pleure, et ars pour ton ingratitude.

MAURICE SCÈVE

371

No longer mourn for me when I am dead,
Than you shall hear the surly sullen bell
Give warning to the world that I am fled
From this vile world with vilest worms to dwell:
Nay if you read this line, remember not
The hand that writ it, for I love you so,
That I in your sweet thoughts would be forgot,
If thinking on me then should make you woe.
O if (I say) you look upon this verse,
When I (perhaps) compounded am with clay,
Do not so much as my poor name rehearse;
But let your love even with my life decay
  Lest the wise world should look into your moan,
  And mock you with me after I am gone.

WILLIAM SHAKESPEARE

372

Past ruin'd Ilion Helen lives,
  Alcestis rises from the shades;
Verse calls them forth; 'tis verse that gives
  Immortal youth to mortal maids.

Soon shall Oblivion's deepening veil
   Hide all the peopled hills you see,
The gay, the proud, while lovers hail
   In distant ages you and me.

The tear for fading beauty check,
   For passing glory cease to sigh;
One form shall rise above the wreck,
   One name, Ianthe, shall not die.

WALTER SAVAGE LANDOR

373

Ah what avails the sceptred race,
   Ah what the form divine!
What every virtue, every grace!
   Rose Aylmer, all were thine.
Rose Aylmer, whom these wakeful eyes
   May weep, but never see,
A night of memories and of sighs
   I consecrate to thee.

WALTER SAVAGE LANDOR

374

Proud word you never spoke, but you will speak
   Four not exempt from pride some future day.
Resting on one white hand a warm wet cheek
   Over my open volume you will say,
   'This man loved *me!*' then rise and trip away.

WALTER SAVAGE LANDOR

375

Twenty years hence my eyes may grow
If not quite dim, yet rather so,
Still yours from others they shall know
                                   Twenty years hence.
Twenty years hence tho' it may hap
That I be call'd to take a nap
In a cool cell where thunder-clap
                                   Was never heard.
There breathe but o'er my arch of grass
A not too sadly sigh'd *Alas,*
And I shall catch, ere you can pass,
                                   That winged word.

WALTER SAVAGE LANDOR

376

Come away, come away death,
And in sad cypress let me laid.
Fly away, fly away breath,
I am slain by a fair cruel maid:
   My shroud of white, stuck all with yew, O prepare it.
   My part of death no one so true did share it.

Not a flower, not a flower sweet
On my black coffin, let there be strown:
Not a friend, not a friend greet
My poor corpse, where my bones shall be thrown:
   A thousand thousand sighs to save, lay me O where
   Sad true lover never find my grave, to weep there.

WILLIAM SHAKESPEARE

Because I liked you better
   Than suits a man to say,
It irked you, and I promised
   To throw the thought away.

To put the world between us
   We parted, stiff and dry;
'Good-bye', said you, 'forget me.'
   'I will, no fear', said I.

If here, where clover whitens
   The dead man's knoll, you pass,
And no tall flower to meet you
   Starts in the trefoiled grass,

Halt by the headstone naming
   The heart no longer stirred,
And say the lad that loved you
   Was one that kept his word.

A. E. HOUSMAN

378 OPHELIA'S SONG

How should I your true love know from another one?
By his cockle hat and staff, and his sandal shoon.

He is dead and gone, lady, he is dead and gone,
At his head a grass-green turf, at his heels a stone.

   White his shroud as the mountain snow,
   Larded with sweet flowers:
   Which bewept to the grave did go,
   With true-love showers.

WILLIAM SHAKESPEARE

379 OPHÉLIE

I

Sur l'onde calme et noire où dorment les étoiles
La blanche Ophélia flotte comme un grand lys,
Flotte très lentement, couchée en ses longs voiles . . .
— On entend dans les bois lointains des hallalis.

Voici plus de mille ans que la triste Ophélie
Passe, fantôme blanc, sur le long fleuve noir.
Voici plus de mille ans que sa douce folie
Murmure se romance à la brise du soir.

Le vent baise ses seins et déploie en corolle
Ses grands voiles bercés mollement par les eaux;
Les saules frissonnants pleurent sur son épaule,
Sur son grand front rêveur s'inclinent les roseaux.

Les nénuphars froissés soupirent autour d'elle;
Elle éveille parfois, dans un aune qui dort,
Quelque nid, d'où s'échappe un petit frisson d'aile:
— Un chant mystérieux tombe des astres d'or.

II

O pâle Ophélia belle comme la neige!
Oui, tu mourus, enfant, par un fleuve emporté!
— C'est que les vents tombant des grands monts de Norwège
T'avaient parlé tout bas de l'âpre liberté;

C'est qu'un souffle, tordant ta grande chevelure,
A ton esprit rêveur portait d'étranges bruits;
Que ton cœur écoutait le chant de la Nature
Dans les plaintes de l'arbre et les soupirs des nuits;

C'est que la voix des mers folles, immense râle,
Brisait ton sein d'enfant, trop humain et trop doux;
C'est qu'un matin d'avril, un beau cavalier pâle,
Un pauvre fou, s'assit muet à tes genoux!

Ciel! Amour! Liberté! Quel rêve, ô pauvre Folle!
Tu te fondais à lui comme une neige au feu;
Tes grandes visions étranglaient ta parole
— Et l'Infini terrible effara ton œil bleu!

III

— Et le Poète dit qu'aux rayons des étoiles
Tu viens chercher, la nuit, les fleurs que tu cueillis,
Et qu'il a vu sur l'eau, couchée en ses longs voiles,
La blanche Ophélia flotter, comme un grand lys.

ARTHUR RIMBAUD

380 TWO WELSH PENILLION

i

THE YEW-TREE

What happiness you gave to me
Underneath this graveyard tree
When in my embraces wound,
Dear heart, you lay above the ground.

ii

THE ROCK

By a flat rock on the shore of the sea
My dear one spoke to me. Wild thyme

Now grows by the rock,
And a sprig of the rosemary.

ANON. (translated by GEOFFREY GRIGSON)

381 COLLOQUE SENTIMENTAL

Dans le vieux parc solitaire et glacé
Deux formes ont tout à l'heure passé.

Leurs yeux sont morts et leur lèvres sont molles,
Et l'on entend à peine leurs paroles.

Dans le vieux parc solitaire et glacé
Deux spectres ont évoqué le passé.

— Te souvient-il de notre extase ancienne?
— Pourquoi voulez-vous donc qu'il m'en souvienne?

— Ton cœur bat-il toujours à mon seul nom?
Toujours vois-tu mon âme en rêve? — Non.

— Ah! les beaux jours de bonheur indicible
Où nous joignions nos bouches! — C'est possible.

— Qu'il etait bleu, le ciel, et grand, l'espoir!
— L'espoir a fui, vaincu, vers le ciel noir.

Tels ils marchaient dans les avoines folles,
Et la nuit seule entendit leurs paroles.

PAUL VERLAINE

Lay a garland on my hearse
   Of the dismal yew;
Maidens, willow branches bear;
   Say I died true.

My Love was false, but I was firm
   From my hour of birth.
Upon my buried body lay
   Lightly, gently, earth.

JOHN FLETCHER

383

Fear no more the heat o' the' sun,
Nor the furious winter's rages,
Thou thy worldly task hast done,
Home art gone, and ta'en thy wages.
Golden lads, and girls all must,
As chimney-sweepers come to dust.

Fear no more the frown o' th' great,
Thou art past the tyrant's stroke,
Care no more to clothe and eat,
To thee the reed is as the oak;
The sceptre, learning, physic must
All follow this, and come to dust.

Fear no more the lightning flash,
Nor th' all-dreaded thunderstone.
Fear not slander, censure rash.
Thou hast finish'd joy and moan.

All lovers young, all lovers must,
Consign to thee and come to dust.

No exorciser harm thee,
Nor no witch-craft charm thee.
Ghost unlaid forbear thee.
Nothing ill come near thee.
Quiet consummation have,
And renowned be thy grave.

WILLIAM SHAKESPEARE

384

Thus sung Orpheus to his strings,
  When he was almost slain,
Whilst the winds, soft murmuring,
  Answered all his woes again:
Ah, dear Eurydice, he cried;
  Ah, dear Eurydice—and so he died.
Ah, dear Eurydice the echoing winds replied.

ANON.

385 THE RELIC

When my grave is broke up again
Some second guest to entertain,
(For graves have learn'd that woman-head
To be to more than one a bed)

And he that digs it, spies
A bracelet of bright hair about the bone,
Will he not let us alone,
And think that there a loving couple lies
Who thought that this device might be some way
To make their souls, at the last busy day,
Meet at this grave, and make a little stay?

If this fall in a time, or land,
Where mis-devotion doth command,
Then, he that digs us up will bring
Us, to the Bishop, and the King,
To make us relics; then
Thou shalt be a Mary Magdalen, and I
A something else thereby;
All women shall adore us, and some men;
And since at such times miracles are sought,
I would have that age by this paper taught
What miracles we harmless lovers wrought.

First, we lov'd well and faithfully,
Yet knew not what we lov'd, nor why;
Difference of sex no more we knew,
Than our guardian angels do;
Coming and going, we
Perchance might kiss, but not between those meals;
Our hands ne'er touch'd the seals,
Which nature, injur'd by late law, sets free:
These miracles we did; but now alas,
All measure, and all language, I should pass,
Should I tell what a miracle she was.

JOHN DONNE

386 AFTER DEATH

The curtains were half drawn, the floor was swept
   And strewn with rushes, rosemary and may
Lay thick upon the bed on which I lay,
Where through the lattice ivy-shadows crept.
He leaned above me, thinking that I slept
   And could not hear him; but I heard him say,
   'Poor child, poor child': and as he turned away
Came a deep silence, and I knew he wept.
He did not touch the shroud, or raise the fold
   That hid my face, or take my hand in his,
     Or ruffle the smooth pillows for my head:
     He did not love me living; but once dead
   He pitied me; and very sweet it is
To know he still is warm though I am cold.

28 *April* 1849.

CHRISTINA ROSSETTI

387 THE CHURCHYARD ON THE
SANDS

My Love lies in the gates of foam,
   The last dear wreck of shore;
The naked sea-marsh binds her home,
   The sand her chamber door.

The gray gull flaps the written stones,
   The ox-birds chase the tide;
And near that narrow field of bones
   Great ships at anchor ride.

Black piers with crust of dripping green,
   One foreland, like a hand,
O'er intervals of grass between
   Dim lonely dunes of sand.

A church of silent weathered looks,
   A breezy reddish tower,
A yard whose mounded resting-nooks
   Are tinged with sorrel flower.

In peace the swallow's eggs are laid
   Along the belfry walls;
The tempest does not reach her shade,
   The rain her silent halls.

But sails are sweet in summer sky,
   The lark throws down a lay;
The long salt levels steam and dry,
   The cloud-heart melts away.

But patches of the sea-pink shine,
   The pied crows poise and come;
The mallow hangs, the bindweeds twine,
   Where her sweet lips are dumb.

The passion of the wave is mute;
   No sound or ocean shock;
No music save the rilling flute
   That marks the curlew flock.

But yonder when the wind is keen,
   And rainy air is clear,
The merchant city's spires are seen,
   The toil of men grows near.

Along the coast-way grind the wheels
   Of endless carts of coal;
And on the sides of giant keels
   The shipyard hammers roll.

The world creeps here upon the shout,
   And stirs my heart in pain;
The mist descends and blots it out,
   And I am strong again.

Strong and alone, my dove, with thee;
   And, tho' mine eyes be wet,
There's nothing in the world to me
   So dear as my regret.

I would not change my sorrow, sweet,
   For others' nuptial hours;
I love the daisies at thy feet
   More than their orange flowers.

My hand alone shall tend thy tomb
   From leaf-bud to leaf-fall,
And wreathe around each season's bloom
   Till autumn ruins all.

Let snowdrops, early in the year,
   Droop o'er her silent breast;
And bid the later cowslip rear
   The amber of its crest.

Come hither, linnets tufted-red,
   Drift by, O wailing tern;
Set pure vale lilies at her head,
   At her feet lady-fern.

Grow, samphire, at the tidal brink,
   Wave, pansies of the shore,
To whisper how alone I think
   Of her for evermore.

Bring blue sea-hollies thorny, keen,
   Long lavender in flower;
Gray wormwood like a hoary queen,
   Stanch mullein like a tower.

O sea-wall mounded long and low
   Let iron bounds be thine;
Nor let the salt wave overflow
   That breast I held divine.

Nor float its sea-weed to her hair,
   Nor dim her eyes with sands:
No fluted cockle burrow where
   Sleep folds her patient hands.

Tho' thy crest feel the wild sea's breath,
   Tho' tide-weight tear thy root,
Oh, guard the treasure house, where Death
   Has bound my darling mute.

Tho' cold her pale lips to reward
   With love's own mysteries,
Ah, rob no daisy from her sward,
   Rough gale of eastern seas!

Ah, render sere no silent bent,
   That by her head-stone waves;
Let noon and golden summer blent
   Pervade these ocean graves.

And, ah, dear heart, in thy still nest,
    Resign this earth of woes,
Forget the ardours of the west,
    Neglect the morning glows.

Sleep, and forget all things but one,
    Heard in each wave of sea,—
How lonely all the years will run
    Until I rest by thee.

JOHN LEICESTER WARREN, LORD DE TABLEY

388

Come not, when I am dead,
    To drop thy foolish tears upon my grave,
To trample round my fallen head,
    And vex the unhappy dust thou wouldst not save.
There let the wind sweep and the plover cry;
    But thou, go by.

Child, if it were thine error or thy crime
    I care no longer, being all unblest:
Wed whom thou wilt, but I am sick of Time,
    And I desire to rest.
Pass on, weak heart, and leave me where I lie;
    Go by, go by.

ALFRED TENNYSON

389 DIRCE

Stand close around, ye Stygian set,
   With Dirce in one boat convey'd,
Or Charon, seeing, may forget
   That he is old, and she a shade.

WALTER SAVAGE LANDOR

390 ON HIS DEAD WIFE

Methought I saw my late espoused saint
   Brought to me like Alcestis from the grave,
   Whom Jove's great son to her glad husband gave,
   Rescued from death by force, though pale and faint.
Mine, as whom washed from spot of childbed taint
   Purification in the old Law did save,
   And such as yet once more I trust to have
   Full sight of her in heaven without restraint,
Came vested all in white, pure as her mind.
   Her face was veiled, yet to my fancied sight
   Love, sweetness, goodness, in her person shined
So clear as in no face with more delight.
   But O as to embrace me she inclined,
   I waked, she fled, and day brought back my night.

JOHN MILTON

391 THE WIND AT THE DOOR

As day did darken on the dewless grass
There still wi' nwone a-come by me,
To staÿ a-while at hwome by me;
Within the house, all dumb by me,
I zot me sad as the eventide did pass.

An' there a win'-blast shook the rattlèn door,
An' seemed, as win' did mwone without,
As if my Jeäne, alwone without,
A-stannèn on the stone without,
Wer there a-come wi' happiness oonce mwore.

I went to door; an' out vrom trees above
My head, upon the blast by me,
Sweet blossoms wer a-cast by me,
As if my love, a-past by me,
Did fling em down—a token ov her love.

'Sweet blossoms o' the tree where I do murn,'
I thought, 'if you did blow vor her,
Vor apples that should grow vor her,
A-vallèn down below vor her,
O then how happy I should zee you kern.'

But no. Too soon I voun' my charm abroke.
Noo comely soul in white like her—
Noo soul a-steppèn light like her—
An' nwone o' comely height like her—
Went by; but all my grief ageän awoke.

WILLIAM BARNES

392 [*from* THE VICTORIES OF LOVE]

Your love lacks joy, your letter says,
Yes; love requires the focal space
Of recollection or of hope,
Ere it can measure its own scope.
Too soon, too soon comes Death to show
We love more deeply than we know!

The rain, that fell upon the height
Too gently to be call'd delight,
Within the dark vale reappears
As a wild cataract of tears;
And love in life should strive to see
Sometimes what love in death would be!
Easier to love, we so should find,
It is than to be just and kind.

COVENTRY PATMORE

393   THE VOICE

Woman much missed, how you call to me, call to me,
Saying that now you are not as you were
When you had changed from the one who was all to me,
But as at first, when our day was fair.

Can it be you that I hear? Let me view you, then,
Standing as when I drew near to the town
Where you would wait for me: yes, as I knew you then,
Even to the original air-blue gown!

Or is it only the breeze, in its listlessness
Travelling across the wet mead to me here,
You being ever consigned to existlessness,
Heard no more again far or near?

Thus I: faltering forward,
Leaves around me falling,
Wind oozing thin through the thorn from norward,
And the woman calling.

THOMAS HARDY

Go to the western gate, Luke Havergal,
There where the vines cling crimson on the wall,
And in the twilight wait for what will come.
The leaves will whisper there of her, and some,
Like flying words, will strike you as they fall;
But go, and if you listen she will call.
Go to the western gate, Luke Havergal—
Luke Havergal.

No, there is not a dawn in eastern skies
To rift the fiery night that's in your eyes;
But there, where western glooms are gathering,
The dark will end the dark, if anything:
God slays Himself with every leaf that flies,
And hell is more than half of paradise.
No, there is not a dawn in eastern skies—
In eastern skies.

Out of a grave I come to tell you this,
Out of a grave I come to quench the kiss
That flames upon your forehead with a glow
That blinds you to the way that you must go.
Yes, there is yet one way to where she is,
Bitter, but one that faith may never miss.
Out of a grave I come to tell you this—
To tell you this.

There is the western gate, Luke Havergal,
There are the crimson leaves upon the wall.
Go, for the winds are tearing them away,—
Nor think to riddle the dead words they say,

Nor any more to feel them as they fall;
But go, and if you trust her she will call.
There is the western gate, Luke Havergal—
Luke Havergal.

EDWIN ARLINGTON ROBINSON

395 IF YOU HAD KNOWN

If you had known
When listening with her to the far-down moan
Of the white-selvaged and empurpled sea,
And rain came on that did not hinder talk,
Or damp your flashing facile gaiety
In turning home, despite the slow wet walk
By crooked ways, and over stiles of stone;
If you had known

You would lay roses,
Fifty years thence, on her monument, that discloses
Its graying shape upon the luxuriant green;
Fifty years thence to an hour, by chance led there,
What might have moved you?—yea, had you foreseen
That on the tomb of the selfsame one, gone where
The dawn of every day is as the close is,
You would lay roses!

THOMAS HARDY

396 AFTER A JOURNEY

Hereto I come to view a voiceless ghost;
  Whither, O whither will its whim now draw me?
Up the cliff, down, till I'm lonely, lost,
  And the unseen waters' ejaculations awe me.

Where you will next be there's no knowing,
  Facing round about me everywhere,
    With your nut-coloured hair,
And gray eyes, and rose-flush coming and going.

Yes: I have re-entered your olden haunts at last;
  Through the years, through the dead scenes I have tracked you;
What have you now found to say of our past—
  Scanned across the dark space wherein I have lacked you?
Summer gave us sweets, but autumn wrought division?
  Things were not lastly as firstly well
    With us twain, you tell?
But all's closed now, despite Time's derision.

I see what you are doing: you are leading me on
  To the spots we knew when we haunted here together,
The waterfall, above which the mist-bow shone
  At the then fair hour in the then fair weather,
And the cave just under, with a voice still so hollow
  That it seems to call out to me from forty years ago,
    When you were all aglow,
And not the thin ghost that I now fraily follow!

Ignorant of what there is flitting here to see,
  The waked birds preen and the seals flop lazily;
Soon you will have, Dear, to vanish from me,
  For the stars close their shutters and the dawn whitens hazily.
Trust me, I mind not, though Life lours,
  The bringing me here; nay, bring me here again!
    I am just the same as when
Our days were a joy, and our paths through flowers.

Pentargon Bay

THOMAS HARDY

Accept, thou shrine of my dead Saint!
Instead of dirges this complaint;
And for sweet flowers to crown thy hearse,
Receive a strew of weeping verse
From thy griev'd friend, whom thou might'st see
Quite melted into tears for thee.

   Dear loss! since thy untimely fate
My task hath been to meditate
On thee, on thee: thou art the book,
The library whereon I look
Though almost blind. For thee (lov'd clay!)
I languish out, not live the day,
Using no other exercise
But what I practise with mine eyes.
By which wet glasses I find out
How lazily time creeps about
To one that mourns: this, only this
My exercise and bus'ness is:
So I compute the weary hours
With sighs dissolved into showers.

   Nor wonder if my time go thus
Backward and most preposterous;
Thou hast benighted me. Thy set
This eve of blackness did beget,
Who wast my day, (though overcast
Before thou had'st thy noon-tide passed)
And I remember must in tears,
Thou scarce had'st seen so many years
As day tells hours. By thy clear sun
My love and fortune first did run;
But thou wilt never more appear
Folded within my hemisphere:
Since both thy light and motion

Like a fled star is fall'n and gone;
And twixt me and my soul's dear wish
The earth now interposed is,
With such a strange eclipse doth make
As ne'er was read in almanake.

I could allow thee for a time
To darken me and my sad clime,
Were it a month, a year, or ten,
I would thy exile live till then;
And all that space my mirth adjourn
So thou wouldst promise to return;
And putting off thy ashy shroud
At length disperse this sorrow's cloud.

But woe is me! the longest date
Too narrow is to calculate
These empty hopes. Never shall I
Be so much blest, as to descry
A glimpse of thee, till that day come
Which shall the earth to cinders doom,
And a fierce fever must calcine
The body of this world, like thine
(My Little World!). That fit of fire
Once off, our bodies shall aspire
To our souls' bliss: then we shall rise,
And view ourselves with clearer eyes
In that calm region, where no night
Can hide us from each other's sight.

Meantime, thou hast her earth: much good
May my harm do thee. Since it stood
With Heaven's will I might not call
Her longer mine, I give thee all
My short-liv'd right and interest
In her, whom living I lov'd best:
With a most free and bounteous grief,
I give thee what I could not keep.

Be kind to her, and prithee look
Thou write into thy Doomsday book
Each parcel of this rarity
Which in thy casket shrin'd doth lie:
See that thou make thy reck'ning straight,
And yield her back again by weight;
For thou must audit on thy trust
Each grain and atom of this dust:
As thou wilt answer Him, that lent,
Not gave thee, my dear monument.

So close the ground, and 'bout her shade
Black curtains draw, my bride is laid.

Sleep on (my love!) in thy cold bed
Never to be disquieted,
My last good night! Thou wilt not wake
Till I thy fate shall overtake:
Till age, or grief, or sickness must
Marry my body to that dust
It so much loves; and fill the room
My heart keeps empty in thy tomb.
Stay for me there; I will not fail
To meet thee in that hollow vale.
And think not much of my delay;
I am already on the way,
And follow thee with all the speed
Desire can make, or sorrows breed.
Each minute is a short degree
And ev'ry hour a step towards thee.
At night when I betake to rest,
Next morn I rise nearer my west
Of life, almost by eight hours' sail,
Than when sleep breath'd his drowsy gale.

Thus from the sun my bottom steers,
And my days' compass downward bears.
Nor labour I to stem the tide,

Through which to thee I swiftly glide.
   'Tis true; with shame and grief I yield,
Thou, like the van, first took'st the field,
And gotten hast the victory
In thus adventuring to die
Before me; whose more years might crave
A just precedence in the grave.
But hark! My pulse, like a soft drum
Beats my approach, tells thee I come;
And slow howe'er my marches be,
I shall at last sit down by thee.
   The thought of this bids me go on,
And wait my dissolution
With hope and comfort. Dear! (forgive
The crime) I am content to live
Divided, with but half a heart,
Till we shall meet and never part.

HENRY KING

398 THE REVENANT

O all ye fair ladies with your colours and your graces,
  And your eyes clear in flame of candle and hearth,
Toward the dark of this old window lift not up your smiling faces,
  Where a Shade stands forlorn from the cold of the earth.

God knows I could not rest for one I still was thinking of;
  Like a rose sheathed in beauty her spirit was to me;
Now out of unforgottenness a bitter draught I'm drinking of,
  'Tis sad of such beauty unremembered to be.

Men all are shades, O Women. Winds wist not of the way they blow.
  Apart from your kindness, life's at best but a snare.

Though a tongue, now past praise, this bitter thing doth say, I
    know
What solitude means, and how, homeless, I fare.

Strange, strange, are ye all—except in beauty shared with her—
    Since I seek one I loved, yet was faithless to in death.
Not life enough I heaped, so thus my heart must fare with her,
    Now wrapt in the gross clay, bereft of life's breath.

WALTER DE LA MARE

399 THE POOR GHOST

'Oh whence do you come, my dear friend, to me,
With your golden hair all fallen below your knee,

And your face as white as snowdrops on the lea,
And your voice as hollow as the hollow sea?'
'From the other world I come back to you:
My locks are uncurled with dripping drenching dew.
You know the old, whilst I know the new:
But to-morrow you shall know this too.'

'Oh not to-morrow into the dark, I pray;
Oh not to-morrow, too soon to go away:
Here I feel warm and well-content and gay:
Give me another year, another day.'

'Am I so changed in a day and a night
That mine own only love shrinks from me with fright,
Is fain to turn away to left or right
And cover up his eyes from the sight?'

'Indeed I loved you, my chosen friend,
I loved you for life, but life has an end;
Through sickness I was ready to tend;
But death mars all, which we cannot mend.

'Indeed I loved you; I love you yet,
If you will stay where your bed is set,
Where I have planted a violet,
Which the wind waves, which the dew makes wet.'

'Life is gone, then love too is gone,
It was a reed that I leant upon:
Never doubt I will leave you alone
And not wake you rattling bone with bone.

'I go home alone to my bed,
Dug deep at the foot and deep at the head,
Roofed in with a load of lead,
Warm enough for the forgotten dead.

'But why did your tears soak through the clay,
And why did your sobs wake me where I lay?
I was away, far enough away:
Let me sleep now till the Judgment Day.'

25 July 1863.

CHRISTINA ROSSETTI

400 AN END

Love, strong as Death, is dead.
Come, let us make his bed
Among the dying flowers:
A green turf at his head;
And a stone at his feet,
Whereon we may sit
In the quiet evening hours.

He was born in the spring,
And died before the harvesting:
On the last warm summer day
He left us; he would not stay
For autumn twilight cold and grey.
Sit we by his grave, and sing
He is gone away.

To few chords and sad and low
Sing we so:
Be our eyes fixed on the grass
Shadow-veiled as the years pass,
While we think of all that was
In the long ago.

5 March 1849.

CHRISTINA ROSSETTI

401

Shall I compare thee to a summer's day?
Thou art more lovely and more temperate:
Rough winds do shake the darling buds of May,
And summer's lease hath all too short a date:
Sometime too hot the eye of heaven shines,
And often is his gold complexion dimm'd;
And every fair from fair sometime declines,
By chance, or nature's changing course untrimm'd;
But thy eternal summer shall not fade,
Nor lose possession of that fair thou ow'st,
Nor shall death brag thou wander'st in his shade,
When in eternal lines to time thou grow'st,
   So long as men can breathe, or eyes can see,
   So long lives this, and this gives life to thee.

WILLIAM SHAKESPEARE

ACKNOWLEDGEMENTS

Permission to use copyright material is gratefully acknowledged to the following:

Mr. Alan Hodge and The Hogarth Press for 'Shepherdess' from *Collected Poems 1905–1953* by Norman Cameron; Mrs. H. M. Davies and Jonathan Cape Ltd. for 'The Visitor' from *The Complete Poems of W. H. Davies*; the Literary Trustees of Walter de la Mare and the Society of Authors for 'The Revenant' from *The Collected Poems of Walter de la Mare 1969*; Faber and Faber Ltd. for 'La Figlia Che Piange' from *Collected Poems 1909–1962* by T. S. Eliot; Editions Gallimard for 'Les Gertrude Hoffman Girls' from *Capitale de la Douleur* by Paul Eluard; Mr. Robert Graves for four poems from *Collected Poems 1965*, 'Song: How Can I Care' from *Poems 1965–68*, and 'With a Gift of Rings' from *Poems 1970–72* by Robert Graves; Colin Smythe Ltd. for 'Donal Oge' by Augusta Gregory; the Trustees of the Hardy Estate, the Macmillan Company of Canada and Macmillan, London and Basingstoke, for seven poems from *Collected Poems* by Thomas Hardy; the Society of Authors for the Estate of A. E. Housman and Jonathan Cape Ltd. for two poems from *Collected Poems* by A. E. Housman; John Murray (Publishers) Ltd. for 'Tam i' the Kirk' from *Songs of Angus* by Violet Jacob; the Society of Authors for the Estate of James Joyce for two poems by James Joyce; Laurence Pollinger Ltd. and the Estate of Mrs. Frieda Lawrence for five poems from *The Complete Poems of D. H. Lawrence* published by William Heinemann Ltd.; Faber and Faber Ltd. for two poems from *The Collected Poems* by Louis MacNeice; Jonathan Cape Ltd. for 'The Riddle' from *Poems* and 'Calypso's Song to Ulysses' from *Ride the Nightmare* by Adrian Mitchell; Faber and Faber Ltd. for two poems from *Collected Shorter Poems* by Ezra Pound; Laurence Pollinger Ltd. for two poems from *Selected Poems* by John Crowe Ransom published by Eyre & Spottiswoode Ltd.; Barrie & Jenkins for four poems by E. J. Scovell; London Magazine for 'Part of Plenty' by Bernard Spencer; Oxford University Press for 'The Vigil of Venus' translated by Allen Tate and included in

The Swimmers and Other Selected Poems; Garnerstone Press for 'Eros d'Aute' from *Selected Poems* by Theodore Wratislaw; to Mr. Leonard Clark and the Trustees of the Andrew Young Estate for two poems by Andrew Young; and to the Oxford University Press for Annihilation' from *Collected Poems* by Conrad Aiken.

While every effort has been made to secure permission, it has in a few cases proved impossible to trace the author or his executor. We apologize for our apparent negligence.

NOTES AND REFERENCES

(For the poems from the sixteenth- and seventeenth-century song-books references are given below to E. A. Fellowes, *English Madrigal Verse*, 3rd edn., 1967, and to Edward Doughtie, *Lyrics from English Airs 1596–1622*, Harvard 1970.)

2. *Death of Eli*, 1921.

3. *Lusty Juventus*, Tudor Facsimile Texts, 1907.

8. *c.* 1632. *Roxburghe Ballads* ii. 639.

13. *Poésies Complètes* 1858. manchy: a rattan litter. bobre: a one-stringed musical instrument made from a calabash. These are two words from Reunion, the French colony in the Indian Ocean where Lecante de Lisle grew up, and which is the setting of the poem.

14. Thomas Ford, *Musicke of Sundrie Kindes*, 1607. Doughtie, p. 277.

19. cheer: fave, countenance.

21. Formerly attributed to Ralegh. A version of Ronsard, *Amours de Cassandre* XX; Gorges substitutes a swan for Ronsard's white bull.

25. The *Pervigilium Veneris*, by an unknown writer of the fourth(?) century A.D. In No. 26 Patmore gives his version of the refrain.

26. *The Angel in the House*, Canto VII. See note on No. 25.

27. Martin Peerson, *Private Musicke* 1620. Fellowes, p. 174.

28. William Corkine, *Ayres*, 1610. Doughtie, p. 336.

37. *Il Pastor Fido*, 1637, Act 3, Scene 5 (translation of Giovan Battista Guarini's *Il Pastor Fido*, 1590).

40. *The Maid in the Mill*, 1647, Act 5, Scene I.

43. *Archiv* 107, 61 (1901), from Harleian MS. 7578. Not (as stated by Chambers and Sidgwick, *Early English Lyrics*, 1907) a 'short extract' from a longer poem, but a song, or part of a song, inserted in a doggerel description of Elizabethan jollifications in Durham on St. Cuthbert's Day—mummers, pipers, dancers, singing, etc.,

> through every streit
> thus can they go

and every man
his horn did blow
tro tro tro tro
ro ro ro ro ro ro
troro tro tro tro

—after which follows this song of the bride.

        bailie: bailiff.
        beareth the bell away: carries off the prize.

47. The track up to the ruins of Montgomery Castle is still illuminated every spring with huge primroses.

50. *The Angel in the House*, close of Canto XI.

51. *Sonnets from the Portuguese*.

52. *The Thracian Wonder*, 1661 (ascribed to Webster and Rowley), Act 1, Scene 1.

55. *Love's Labour's Lost*, Act 4, Scene 3.

56. *The Winter's Tale*, Act 4, Scene 4.

57. Sixteenth century, from the Bannatyne MS., Scottish Text Society.

58. *Death of Eli*, 1921.

59. pale: pall, mantle.
spangs: spangles.
felter'd: felted, matted.
travesing: traversing.

62. The Fourth Song in *Astrophel and Stella*.

63. *The Two Gentlemen of Verona*, Act 1, Scene 3.

65. *Menaphon*, 1589.

68. *Greenes Mourning Garment*, 1590.

69. *Songs of Angus*, 1915.

70. An expansion of Sappho 90:

    Sweet mother, I cannot work the loom
    Tender Aphrodite subdues me so with longing for a boy.

73. Ault, *Seventeenth Century Lyrics*, 1928. (Bodley MS. Malone 13.)

80. *The Rape of Lucrece*, 1630.

81. avisiness: deliberation.

82. John Farmer, *The First Set of English Madrigals*, 1599. Fellowes, p. 104.

84. Thomas Morley's *Firste Booke of Ayres*, 1600. Fellowes, p. 623.

88. Nicholas Yonge, *Musica Transalpina*, 1588. Fellowes, p. 326.

89. In many parts of France periwinkle is as common in woods and copses in the still leafless spring as primroses in England. See also No. 122 and note.

97. Based on a French *chanson*.
    coy: stroke.

103. Cean Dubh Deelish: dear black head.

105. distain: cause to look pale.
    chere: expression, look.

107. The first stanza is a version of Catullus's *Vivamus, mea Lesbia*.

110. *Alexander and Campaspe*, 1632.

111. *The Merchant of Venice*, Act 5, Scene 1.

115. John Wilson, *Cheerful Ayres or Ballads*, 1660.

118. John Wilbye, *First Set of English Madrigals*, 1598. A translation of Guarini's *Dice la mia bellissima*, from *Rime*, 1598 (Fellowes, p. 306).

120. *The House of Life*, LXIX.

121. *The Angel in the House*, Canto VII.

122. Periwinkle was regarded in the Middle Ages and after as a venereal plant. It was eaten to increase love and appetite between husband and wife. See also No. 89.

126. *The Mad Lover*, 1647, Act 4, Scene 1.

127. *The Angel in the House*, Preludes.

128. *The Temple of Glas*; a *balade simple*, i.e. without an envoi.
    persant: piercing.
    glad: shining.
    price: honour, glory.
    willy: kindly, benevolent.
    gladding: brightening.
    twin: part.

129. *The Angel in the House*, Canto XI.

133. *The Mad Lover*, 1647, Act 4, Scene 1.

134. *The Thracian Wonder*, 1661 (ascribed to Webster and Rowley), Act 2, Scene 1.

135. Thomas Morley, *Madrigalls to Foure Voyces*, 1594, from the first stanza of an Italian poem by Livio Celiano (Fellowes, p. 139).

137. Michael Cavendish, *14 Ayres*, 1598.
    O deus, deus, etc.: 'O God, God, there is no grief like my grief', adapted from the Lamentations of Jeremiah, 1, 12, in the Latin of the Vulgate (Doughtie, p. 90).

139. ourhailit: overwhelmed.

140. *Carolina; or, Loyal Poems*, 1683.

143. *England's Helicon*, 1600.

146. *Fidessa, More Chaste Than Kind*, 1596.

147. *The Chances*, 1647, Act 3, Scene 2.

149. John Wilbye, *The Second Set of Madrigales*, 1609. Fellowes, p. 311.

153. Richard Alison, *An Houres Recreation in Musicke*, 1606. Fellowes, p. 12.

154. c. 1580. Printed in *A Handeful of Pleasant Delites*, 1584.

155. Nicholas Yonge, *Musica Transalpina: The Second Booke of Madrigalles*, 1597.

156. *Sonnets pour Hélène*, 2ᵉ *Livre*.

159. William Corkine, *Ayres, To Sing and Play to the Lute*, 1610. Doughtie, p. 337.
    carted: publicly trundled round in a cart as a whore.

160. *The Spanish Bawd*, 1631 (from the *Comedia de Calisto y Melibea*, by Francisco de Rojas).

170. A version of Petrarch's Sonnet 189.

173. or: ere, before.

174. *Noli me tangere*: touch me not.
    Caesar's I ame: the hind is Henry VIII's Anne Boleyn.

180. John Bartlet, *A Booke of Ayres*, 1606. Doughtie, p. 244.

181. A version of sonnet VIII, 2ᵉ *Livre, Les Amours de Diane*, 1573, by Philippe Desportes (1546–1606): 'Je me veux rendre Hermite, et faire penitence.'

188. *A discourse of the adventures passed by Master F. J.*, in *A Hundreth Sundrie Flowres*, 1573.

189. trentals: sets of thirty masses for the repose of souls of the dead.

190. *Latine Songs and Poems*, 1685.

194. A version of the Provençal alba (twelfth–thirteenth century) 'En un vergier sotz folha d'albespi'.

197. Tobias Hume, *The First Part of Ayres*, 1605. Doughtie, p. 199.

198. *Becket*, Act 2, Scene 1.

200. Fronleichnam: Corpus Christi.

202. John Attey, *The First Booke of Ayres*, 1622. Based on a French song shortened and improved by the translator (Doughtie, p. 415).

211. *Authorized Version* of the Bible, 1611.

212. *Sonnets pour Hélène*, 2ᵉ *Livre*.

214. Ibid.

221. John Dowland, *The First Book of Songs or Ayres*, 1597 (Doughtie, p. 75, with slight changes from *England's Helicon*, 1600).

222. *Troilus and Cressida*, Act 1, Scene 1.

223. *Romeo and Juliet*, Act 3, Scene 2.

224. Robert Jones, *A Musicall Dreame*, 1609. Doughtie, p. 326.

227. Fourteenth century. Bodley MS. Rawlinson D 913, just decipherable on its darkened parchment. Modernized from the transcription in R. H. Robbins, *Secular Lyrics of the XIVth and XVth Centuries*, 1952. As remarkable a fragment(?) surely as the more famous *Westron Wind*, No. 270 ii.

229. Title from Sappho 40:
>   Now Love that dissolves the limbs shakes me,
>   Sweetly bitter unvanquishable creeping thing.

231. *Tragical History of Doctor Faustus*.

251. The shorter (and earlier) version from Puttenham's *Arte of English Poesie*, 1589.

256. In the MS. (Bodleian. Ashm. 38 f. 77) said to have been written by Drayton the night before he died.

259. John Dowland, *The Third and Last Booke of Songs or Aires*, 1603. Doughtie, p. 178.

266. *Poems*, 1664.

267. *Poems*, ed. W. A. Ringler, 1962. But without all the editor's emendations aimed at correcting Sidney's sapphic metre.
persers: piercers.
rehearsers: those who are always repeating in their talk.
swerved: forsaken, avoided.

270. i. Late thirteenth–early fourteenth century. G. L. Brook, *The Harley Lyrics*, 1948. Written out in the MS. (British Museum,

Harley 2253) as the burden to a dissimilar poem. Either a song fragment or possibly (Dronke, *Medieval Latin and the Rise of European Love-Lyric*, 1968, i. 125) 'a traditional song, complete in itself'.

ii. Early sixteenth century. Chambers and Sidgwick, *Early English Lyrics*, 1907. A fragment of a night-visit song recovered in modern form from a Dorset singer (59A in James Reeves, *The Everlasting Circle*, 1960). See A. L. Lloyd, *Folk Song in England*, 1967.

273. *Tottel's Miscellany*, 1557.

276. William Byrd, *Psalms, Sonets and Songs of sadnes and pietie*, 1588. From Ovid's *Heroides* i (Fellowes, p. 48).

287. *Choice Drollery*, 1656.

289. preve: prove.

290. *Roxburghe Ballads*, ed. Chappell and Ebsworth I, 454, reprinted with another version in *Bishop Percy's Folio Manuscript: Loose and Humorous Songs*, ed. F. J. Furnivall, 1868.

294. The title is from Horace, *Odes*, 4. 1.

> *Intermissa, Venus, diu*
> *rursus bella moves. parce, precor, precor.*
> *non sum qualis eram bonae*
> *sub regno Cinarae.*

> Venus, you'd start up the long
> abandoned wars again. No, no, I beg you.
> I am not what I was when
> gentle Cinara reigned.

298. For the title see Euripides, *Hippolytus* 538: Ἔρως τύραννος ἀνδρῶν, 'Love absolute ruler of men'.

299. *Modern Love*, XLV.

307. *The Thracian Wonder*, 1661 (ascribed to Webster and Rowley), Act 1, Scene 1.

319. *The Captain*, 1647. Act 3, Scene 4. Lelia asks for it as 'the sad song'.

320. wait: wot.
deid: death.
sichis: sighs.
wilsome: dreary.

thirlit: pierced.

sea: send.

322. *The House of Life*, LIII.

326. *Becket*, Prologue.

328. Monna Innominata, the Lady Unnamed. The quotations above the sonnets are from Dante, *Purgatorio* VIII, 1 ('It was the hour that reverses the desire of those who go to sea and melts the heart'); Petrarch, *Sonnet XX* ('I come back to the time when I saw you first'); Dante, *Paradiso* III, 85 ('In his will is our peace'), and Petrarch, *Sonetti e Canzoni* XXX ('Alone with these thoughts, with leafage changed').

333. Title: 'The girl who weeps.'
O quam te memorem virgo: Virgil, *Aeneid* 1. 327. 'O what shall I call you, lady' (Aeneas encounters, but does not recogize, his mother Venus).

334. trad the trace: trod the path. moo: more.

337. Mid-fifteenth century. R. H. Robbins, *Secular Lyrics of the XIVth and XVth Centuries, No. 23*.
undo: undone.
y-do: done.
saws: promises.

340. pretence: intention.
laid his faith to borrow: pledged or pawned his word.

342. This and the following three poems are printed in dated sequence in Christina Rossetti's *Collected Poems*, edited by her brother, William Michael Rossetti, who must have known all the circumstances in which they were written. I have left the first of the poems without its title 'Lady Montrevor'. This seems to have been only a device by which Christina Rossetti separated the poem from herself.

349. Francis Pilkington, *The First Booke of Songs*, 1605. Fellowes, p. 636; Doughtie, p. 228.

351. lever: liefer, more acceptable.

353. *Modern Love* XI and XII.

355. Based on Ronsard's famous poem, No. 36, p. 54.

358. *Modern Love* XLIII.

361. *Modern Love* XXIX and XXX.

368. *Délie* 1544, dizaine CCCLXXVIII.
custodes curtains.
heur: happiness, freedom.

370. *Délie* 1544, dizaine LCCCXLVII.
(j') ars: (I) burn.

380. Seventeenth century. T. J. Jones *Penillion Telyn*. The *penill* is a traditional four-line song which was sung to the harp.

382. *The Maides Tragedy*, 1619. Act 2, Scene 1.

384. Walter Porter, *Madrigales and Ayres*, 1632. Fellowes, p. 647.

392. *The Victories of Love*, Book II, V.

INDEX OF POETS AND POEMS

INDEX OF FIRST LINES